PIKE WATERS

AN EXPERT GUIDE TO PIKE FISHING

IN GREAT BRITAIN AND IRELAND

To Liz with love

Illustrations

Contents

First published 1990 by The Boydell Press, Woodbridge

The Boydell Press is an imprint of Boydell & Brewer Ltd
PO Box 9, Woodbridge, Suffolk IP12 3DF

ISBN 0 85115 260 0

British Library Cataloguing in Publication Data
Pike waters : an expert guide to pike fishing in Great Britain and Ireland.
1. Great Britain. Pike. Spinfishing
I. Winship, Bill
799.1753
ISBN 0-85115-260-0

This publication is printed on acid-free paper

Printed in Great Britain by
Dotesios Printers Ltd, Trowbridge, Wiltshire

PIKE WATERS

AN EXPERT GUIDE TO PIKE FISHING IN GREAT BRITAIN AND IRELAND

Edited by
BILL WINSHIP

THE BOYDELL PRESS

Acknowledgements

The outsider may be forgiven for thinking that a book of this nature could be written in a few weeks. In reality it has taken five years to research, to select the right areas and to find anglers with the appropriate knowledge. Meeting and working with these anglers has been a real pleasure and I would like to thank the following people for making this book possible; Dr Barrie Rickards, Dan Leary, John McAngus, Malcolm Bannister, Colin Dyson, Bill Little, Martin Gay, George Sharman and Liz Winship. Special thanks are also due to Fred Buller for his advice on the MS and to Richard Barber, Helen Barber and Pru Harrison from Boydell and Brewer Ltd. Last but by no means least I would like to acknowledge Lee Maloney, Kevin Russell, Dave Tipping, Dennis Winship and David Hall for their photographs and general help.

Bill Winship
10 February 1990

Foreword

The true lover of angling books is a born optimist. Naïvely, he awaits newly published works with the hope of the gambler turning a card. Unlike the gambler, who cares only for material gain, a pay-out of only *one* compelling line would be reward enough.

This book on pike angling, by nine established fishermen who have a special knowledge of the sport in particular regions, covering the greater part of Britain and Ireland, not only confers on its readers a host of compelling lines, delineating what is common to the experience of pike anglers in all those regions, but, more importantly, what is particular.

The dénouement of this book, published at a time when there are more really clever pike fishermen in the British Isles than ever before, is in its simple inference – namely, that none of us is half ready to be described as truly expert, until he has mastered the problems associated with fishing for pike in all the regions. In this book the reader avoids the repetitive descriptions of well known pike angling techniques – because they are absent, as are the cloying details of personal catch records.

That which is on offer is in the long run infinitely more satisfying and enduring because it attempts to cope with the problems associated with catching pike from those distant and romantic 'frontier waters' which have as yet received scant attention.

Bill Winship is responsible for soliciting authors to do this job. He has chosen well. His enthusiasm for the task has inspired his team to produce a book that one day may be seen as a land mark in the slow but ever-swelling library of fine pike angling literature.

Fred Buller

Preface

One of the primary aims of writing this book has been to provide a basic guide to pike fishing in Britain and Ireland. For obvious reasons such an ambitious project could never be attempted by a single author, and this is why specialist knowledge has been collected from a team of Britain's top pike experts. Each writer has been asked to describe the waters they know best and draw out the characteristics which make their waters unique. Different waters present the angler with different problems and wherever necessary advice is given about the methods and techniques needed to overcome local angling problems.

Each one of the ten main chapters represents a separate study of the pike and reflects ten different perspectives on the pike in Great Britain and Ireland. This approach highlights the wide range of conditions in which the pike lives and informs the angler about the best techniques to use within each area. Details are also given on current attitudes to the pike, the effects of pike culling and various other 'human' factors affecting the pike fishing in Britain and Ireland.

Introduction

Over the last fifteen years or so there has been a marked increase in the number of books and journals dealing with the subject of coarse fishing. This growth of interest has been further fuelled by a similar expansion in a number of conservation groups which have brought a more enlightened approach to our sport.

The Pike Anglers Club in particular has brought an air of respectability into pike fishing, which had for too long been regarded as the 'coarsest of coarse fishing'. Now, as a result of these changing attitudes, the pike is one of the most popular species in England, and a number of excellent books have been published about it. Most of these books have dealt primarily with the tackle and techniques required to catch pike. This book is slightly different in the sense that the main weight of emphasis has been centred on discussing pike in relation to the waters in which they live. It has always been known that pike are well distributed across Britain and Ireland, yet variations in the pike's habitat from, say, the Norfolk Broads to the western loughs in the Irish Republic have always been a stumbling block to the adventurous angler. The changes in mental attitude and technique required to master the new found conditions are all too often overwhelming, and whilst such and such an angler may be considered expert on his home ground, his much prized skills may amount to next to nothing when he is faced with a new and unknown water. This fact points to one basic truth about pike fishing, namely that no single individual, no matter how experienced, can ever be considered 'expert' at fishing on all waters. Pike fishing is a broad subject, as wide ranging in scope as the waters which contain our quarry. As a consequence, for the pike angler, life is all too short; it only allows each individual sufficient time to sample a tiny fraction of what is available to him. Yet we do know that it is quite possible for an angler to become familiar with one water system and to know it well enough to be able to excel in all kinds of conditions. This book has been written by anglers who understand their waters in this intimate way, from knowledge gleaned over many years. Ten distinct regions are covered, varying from fast moorland streams to the sluggish waters of the Norfolk Broads. The differences between the various regions are great, and it is remarkable how the pike can thrive in so many varying habitats. Essentially this is a study in the distribution of a species, and a study in contrast. It is this variability within the species and its surroundings which makes the pike such an interesting fish to pursue and this book has been compiled with the intention of revealing a little of what is available to the travelling angler.

In the first section John McAngus has described the Fenland drain system which is one of the most prolific in Britain. John is widely recognised as one of the leading authorities on the Fens and has unique access to a whole range of information on the area. This chapter represents one of the most authoritative accounts ever written on the Fenland drain system.

As a complete contrast to the Fenlands, the English Lake District has been dealt with by Malcolm Bannister, the well known Pike Anglers Club secretary. Malcolm has fished the mountain lakes of Cumbria for many years and describes how to set about the difficult task of finding where, when and how to catch hard-fighting mountain pike.

Although I have fished for pike in most parts of Britain and the Irish Republic, I understand my local 'fast-river pike' better than any others. In the Yorkshire chapter I describe the unique characteristics of fast-river pike and explain about the harsh conditions which make these fish some of the most hard fighting pike of all. The fast-river section has been written in conjunction with the slow-river section, both of which describe parts of the Yorkshire Ouse catchment area. This dual approach to river pike helps to highlight the sheer contrast between fish from different areas along the same river course.

The series of interconnected rivers and lakes collectively known as the Norfolk Broads represents some of the most interesting waters as far as pike fishing is concerned. This important section has been dealt with by Dan Leary who has spent many years on these waters as bailiff and angler. Dan's understanding of this complex system of dykes, broads and rivers is very illuminating and is aimed at providing the visitor with a headstart in fishing these extensive waters.

Across that narrow strip of water known as the Irish Sea lies one of the most interesting pike fisheries of all. Although through frustration many English pikemen have turned their attentions away from the Emerald Isle there is no denying that it has an unequalled history in terms of its potential for producing very big pike. Ireland presents the pike angler with the ultimate test to his enthusiasm and skill. Ireland can be a heart breaker, yet it can also produce results like nowhere else on Earth. Part of the answer to a successful trip lies in preparation and knowing where to go. For this reason the first part of this section is based on preparation. In the second part Barrie Rickards concentrates on the group of loughs known collectively as the western fisheries of Ireland. These are the waters which have produced over fifty pike upwards of 35 lb and still provide good sport for those willing to try. Barrie has written extensively on Irish pike and there can be few people better qualified to offer advice on the subject. On the giant Irish loughs like Mask, Corrib and Conn fish location can be a major problem, even for local anglers. However, with the help of the modern depth-sounding devices the problems of location can be greatly simplified. In the final part of the Irish section Colin Dyson describes how modern equipment can be put to good use in finding pike.

Most of the people who write about the Scottish pike scene come from England. This situation has come about for the simple reason that most Scottish anglers prefer salmon and trout to pike. Bill Little, however, is a now not-so-rare exception to this rule. Bill lives in Glasgow and has fished for big loch pike for over fifteen years now, not as a tourist, but as a local angler. Bill's understanding of loch pike is amply demonstrated by his results which have been achieved by fishing the lochs all the year round.

To some anglers those great sheets of water known as reservoirs and gravel pits present a great enigma. The sheer size of these waters can be off-putting but in this section Martin Gay has shown that even the seemingly featureless reservoirs can succumb to intelligent analysis. Martin is one of the most respected pike anglers in the country and has written extensively on the subject of pike.

It was only a few years ago that pike in the 20–30 lb bracket started to be caught from a whole series of lakes not previously known to yield big pike. These new lakes had one thing in common, namely they had all been stocked with rainbow trout. As each year passes the pike from these waters seem to get bigger and bigger. Now people are beginning to question how long it will be before fish in the 50–60 lb class will be caught. I have made a study of these fish and describe some of the factors affecting growth limits in these waters.

No book on the subject of pike would be complete without some reference to growth and seasonal feeding habits of the species. On the subject of growth, the well known author George Sharman has made an in-depth study on the age, weight and growth of the pike. He has also provided details and instructions on the subject of scale interpretation; these writings represent the fruits of many years' work on the subject and have never been published before.

In the closing chapter I deal with the important subject of weather and season. I start by explaining the way in which pike are affected by weather conditions, and go on to describe on a month-by-month basis how pike are affected by seasonal change. This chapter takes the form of a pike anglers' calendar and provides a useful guide to those who choose to fish for pike all the year round.

AUTHORS

1. John McAngus	Fenland Pike
2. Malcolm Bannister	Mountain Lakes of Cumbria
3. Bill Winship	Yorkshire River Pike
4. Dan Leary	Norfolk Pike
5. Bill Winship	Irish Waters
6. Barrie Richards	The Western Loughs of Ireland
7. Bill Little	Scottish Lochs
8. Martin Gay	Reservoirs and Gravel Pits

Fenland Pike

JOHN McANGUS

In a massive arc around the Wash lies the great Fenland plain. Of the total area of England and Wales only five per cent is classified as first class agricultural land, and almost the whole of the Fenland falls into this category. But it is not only fruit and vegetables that are harvested here, for the area has always been noted for its fishing. The centre of the fens is Ely, which means Eel Island. Before the fens were drained in the middle of the seventeenth century, many parishioners paid their tithes to the church in eels. Fish were an important part of the livelihood of the old fenmen and they reacted violently to the drainage works, often sabotaging sluices and embankments. But eventually the huge swamp was drained thanks to a complex network of drains and dykes, which still contained plenty of fish. Eel fishermen using nets and traps continued to reap a rich harvest, but the area was little fished with rod and line until after the First World War. With better road and rail transport matchmen from the Midlands and the north, especially Sheffield, discovered the rich potential of the Fens.

It was, however, very recently, from about the mid-sixties in fact, that anglers realised that the Fens could provide superb Pike-fishing. Up to then pike were mostly caught for the pot, by simple methods like bung-fishing with live baits, and spinning, usually with bar-spoons. Nonetheless some huge fish were occasionally caught; the best, from Vandervells Lake near Welney, (not really a Fen drain fish) weighed 36 lb 8 oz and was taken in 1957 on a livebait by Col. H. Atherton. The fish was mounted and can still be seen at the Lamb and Flag pub in Welney. Another huge fish was taken by Great Ouse bailiffs in the same year, by electro-fishing from the Old Bedford River near Manea. It weighed 36 lbs, and was released alive.

In the early 1960s developments took place which were to have far reaching consequences for fishing in the Fens. Firstly two major drains were cut and filled with water. It is interesting to note that both had formed part of the original drainage plans of Sir Cornelius Vermuyden in the 1650s, but it was three hundred years before they were actually dug out. The Relief Channel was the major drain running 11 miles from Denver to King's Lynn. This massive water is over 100 yards wide for

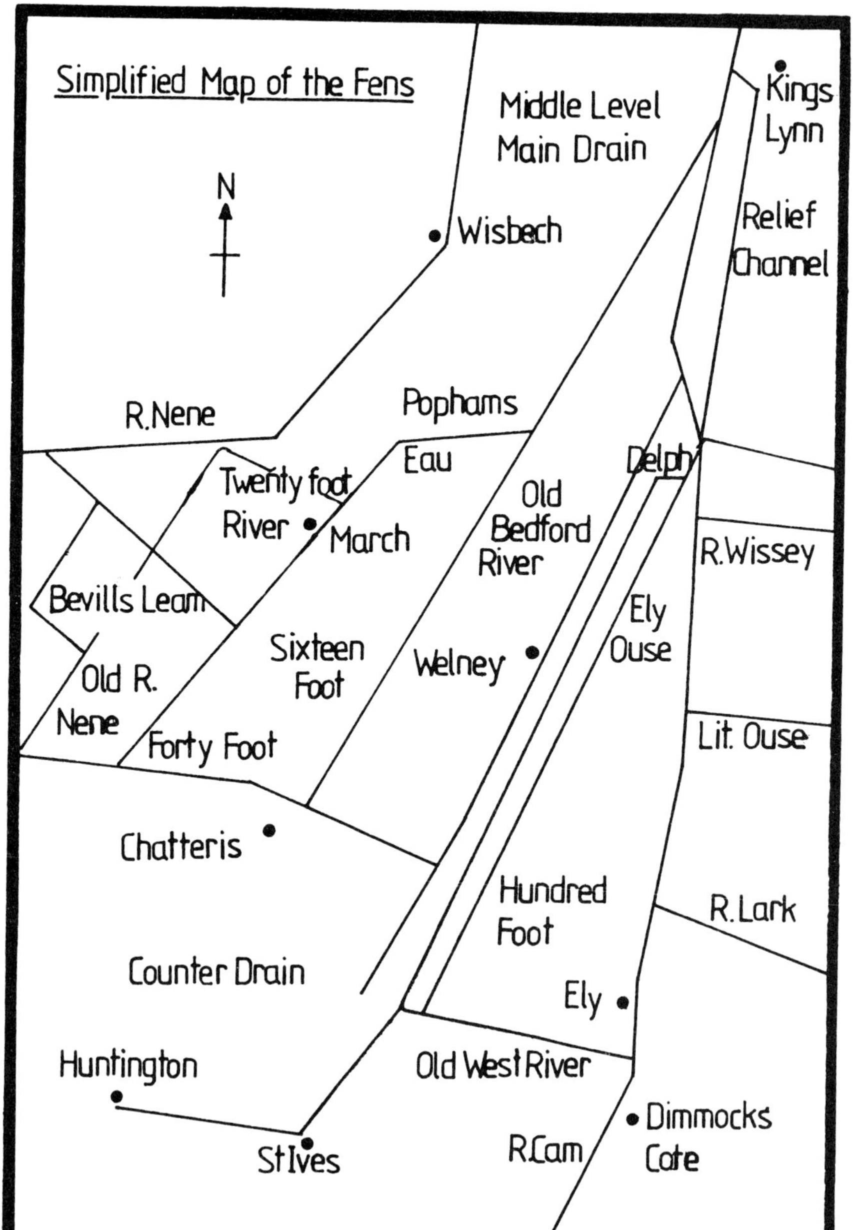

Simplified Map of the Fens
N
Middle Level
Main Drain
Kings
Lynn
Wisbech
Relief
Channel
R.Nene
Pophams
Eau
Delph
Twenty foot
River
March
Old
Bedford
River
R.Wissey
Bevills Leam
Ely
Ouse
Sixteen
Foot
Welney
Old R.
Nene
Forty Foot
Lit. Ouse
Chatteris
Hundred
Foot
R.Lark
Counter Drain
Ely
Huntington
Old West River
Dimmocks
Cote
St Ives
R.Cam
Cambridge

much of its length, with its sister water, the Cut-off Channel, running nearly 30 miles from Mildenhall to Denver. The Relief Channel was to be the Great Ouse River Board's showpiece fishery and so between 1960 and 1964, when it was opened for fishing, a massive re-stocking took place. Over 100,000 fish were put into the virgin water, mostly roach and bream, but on 18 March 1963 ninety-seven Zander were also released at Stowbridge, the significance of which would take some years to become apparent.

The new channel produced staggering match fishing results, with catches over 50 lb quite commonly taken, and at about the same time local anglers discovered that it also contained some fabulous pike. Ray Webb, Barrie Rickards, Bill Chillingsworth and Hugh Reynolds formed the nucleus of the Cambridgeshire Pike Angling Club, who were rapidly improving their fishing techniques and making terrific catches. The fish were young, fat and big. A classic example is Ray's twenty pounder that was just 34 in long. The prospects looked excellent.

It was about this time that I moved to live in the Fens (because the fishing was so good) and in 1970 I obtained a job with the Great Ouse River Authority as a water bailiff. It was like a dream come true. Every day was spent on the river bank either netting, electro-fishing, or carrying out licence checking patrols. The area was very very popular with anglers – in 1974 I carried out a survey which showed that over 54,000 anglers were fishing my 'patch'.

At about the time I started as a bailiff the pike fishing groups began to explore the Fenland system in earnest. In subsequent years the news of big catches acted like a magnet and pike specialists came to the area in ever increasing numbers. Few weeks passed without reports of twenty pounders in the press and I frequently witnessed the capture of large pike during my patrols. The early breakthroughs came on Bevills Leam and the Twenty Foot River where fish to 26 lb were taken. Towards the end of 1971 the Sixteen Foot Drain came to prominence, producing six fish over 20 lb and one monster of 31 lb 8 oz to Northampton's Bob Church. All these fish came from a tiny 200 yard long hotspot at Jenny Gray's farm. During 1972 the River Delph below Welney began to show promise. It had been severely polluted five years previously, but had recovered astonishingly quickly, and it soon became apparent that the four and a quarter mile stretch held a large number of very big fish. This promise was realised to the full in the first twelve weeks of 1973 with twenty-one pike over 20 lb topped by a magnificent thirty-three pounder.

1973 was an exceptional year for big fish, for in addition to the 'thirty-three' the Delph produced fish of 28 lb 14 oz and 28 lb 12 oz, and the Sixteen Foot was again well represented with fish of 29 lb, 27 lb 8 oz and 27 lb 1 oz. The Twenty Foot and Bevills Leam produced a 29 lb fish, a 28 lb 12 oz pike was taken from the Hundred Foot, and the tiny

John McAngus with a 22 lb 12 oz pike taken from the River Delph on New Year's Day 1976. (Photo: J. McAngus)

Old River Nene at Ramsey came up with two fish weighing 29 lb 8 oz and 28 12 oz.

As reports of these catches filtered through the number of anglers visiting the area solely in search of pike doubled almost overnight. The pressure on the pike stocks of the Fens intensified to a degree unimaginable three years previously.

1974 catches slumped, mainly due to atrocious weather, as gale force winds and heavy rain lashed the area through the latter months of the year and many drains were unfishable due to pumping. In early 1975 I produced a few statistics of the big pike for *Anglers' Mail* which showed what a fantastic period of pike angling it had been.

The information was obtained as follows.

(a) Fish witnessed personally	67
(b) Press reports	85
(c) Information from reliable sources	44

Pike over 20 lb
1 January 1970 to 31 December 1974

Name of water	*1970*	*1971*	*1972*	*1973*	*1974*	*Total*
Sixteen Foot Drain	5	14	10	7	6	42
Old Bedford/R.Delph	–	–	7	24	–	31
Twenty Foot River	4	5	6	5	2	22
Bevills Leam	6	5	2	2	3	18
Middle Level Main Drain	3	2	3	3	6	17
Counter Wash/Old Bedford	6	–	1	–	7	14
Yaxley Drains	3	3	4	2	1	13
Old River Nene	1	–	1	3	1	6
Various minor drains	5	4	5	4	2	20
Various stillwaters	4	3	3	2	1	13
Totals	37	36	42	52	29	196

The results during 1975 and 1976 were dreadful and by November 1976 an article I wrote for *Anglers' Mail* indicated a very different picture. On one known spawning site no more than eighty Pike were actively spawning in 1976 compared with over two hundred in 1971. Anglers reported a marked decline in their catches of pike, and I argued that there had been no sign of reducing pike stocks until the Fens came in for intensive fishing. Groups of anglers camped out at hotspots for several days, fishing around the clock, sometimes using multiple rods; four or five, or even six, rods per angler was not unusual. Often these rods were left poorly attended and one angler might be left watching twelve lots of tackle when his companions had gone to explore (often the pubs!). Poor handling of fish was common and so any Fenland pike that was unlucky enough to be caught still had to endure several hours in a keepnet, or attached to a large safety pin device called a stringer, before being photographed and returned to the water . . . where he was immediately fished for again. Two examples come to mind.

List of 30 lb pike taken 1944–1974

lbs oz	*Water*	*Captor*	*Year*
36 08	Vandervells Lake	Col. H. Atherton	1957
36 00	Old Bedford River	Electro-fishing	1957
33 00	River Delph	David Malin	1973
33 00	Sixteen Foot	Anon.	1957
31 08	Sixteen Foot	Bob Church	1971

On the River Delph late one Sunday afternoon I came across three rods, and could see no sign of an angler. I noticed a run develop on one rod and after a few moments struck into a heavy fish, by this time a figure could be seen in the distance running towards me. I played, beat, and saw the fish in what seemed about the five minutes that it took the angler to reach me. As he arrived I allowed the fish to sound so he could not see its size and asked him if it was to be his fish or mine. His, he gasped, so I handed him the rod and twenty seconds later I netted a superb 28 lb 14 oz pike for him. Later we exchanged sharp words.

The second example was during a patrol along the Twenty Foot River when I met an old hand at fishing the drains. He had noticed that catches were not so good, but he had been fishing the area for over ten years, averaging about twenty double-figure fish per season. Unfortunately he had never caught a 'twenty'. His best fish had weighed just over 17 lb. Nonetheless he was very happy with his results. Later the same day I met a young lad at Goosetree Corner who had travelled from the Midlands to fish the Fens on four occasions. He felt he was a failure, because every week he read of 'twenties' and his best catch in four days was a poor seventeen pounder. The contrast was so sharp I began to think that pike anglers had somehow lost their way, and some

Stop netting during an electro-fishing survey on the Fens. Left to right: John McAngus, Chris Klee, Don Prior. (Photo: J. McAngus)

Bailiffs electro-fishing a Fenland river. Left to right: 'Binks' Cottrell on the bank, John McAngus, Don Priory, Doug Yates. (Photo: J. McAngus)

of their values. I wrote a rude article in *Anglers' Mail* blaming intensive fishing for the decline in pike catches. Perhaps it did have an effect. I am still convinced it did, but events were to indicate that something much more radical was wrong in the Fens.

It began in 1977 when the bottom dropped out of the previously superb match fishing. Good catches, once common, now became so scarce that the flow of 54,000 anglers slowed and almost stopped. Results were so bad that several 30 peg matches ended with no fish caught at all, a situation unthinkable ten years previously.

The Fisheries Department was also going through a period of considerable change, the old fashioned 'rule of thumb' Fisheries Officers were being replaced by a new breed of fishery worker, the scientist. Their approach was very different in that they began a series of surveys throughout the area, with particular note taken of the Fens. The surveys consisted of electro-fishing and netting of lengths of rivers or drains, estimating the fish population in that section, and then extrapolating the results for the whole length of the waterway. The results were startling, and showed clearly that waters which held established populations of zander were markedly different from those with no zander.

Predator prey ratios 1979/80

Water	*Period of zander colonisation (Years)*	*Predators (i.e. pike & zander) % of total population*
Relief Channel	16	80
Middle Level Main Drain	10	50
Old West River	10	37
Twenty Foot River	4	34
Kings Dyke	1	28
Middle Witham and River Till	0	6

A number of anglers suggested that zander were being used as a scapegoat but the exact coincidence of the huge imbalance between predator and prey is unlikely to have arisen by chance, and a cause-effect link certainly existed.

The scientific literature and the result of our surveys showed that these fisheries could sustain a population of predators occupying up to about 20 to 25 per cent of the total population by weight. If the predators occupied more than this proportion of the population, then there was a very real danger that insufficient young prey fish would survive long enough to reach maturity and breed. A full population 'crash' had therefore occurred in the Relief Channel, and was in progress throughout the Middle Level system of drains. It was clear that something had to be done to remove zander, and to try to stop the species extending its range.

Water bailiffs began at once to try to remove zander using gill nets and other traps, but these caused too much damage to other species. We also tried to stop the zander reaching the Nene system by regularly electro-fishing the Kings Dyke and removing them. We even considered chlorination at Stanground Lock, but this caused too many other problems, and eventually zander did manage to evade our electro-fishing and move into the River Nene.

By contrast to our own attempts to remove zander, anglers were outstandingly successful at removing the species by rod and line. It does not take too much imagination to see why. The zander and pike were very short of food, so anglers' baits were more than welcome. We tried to enlist the co-operation of local and visiting anglers to cull zander by rod and line. Anglers responded magnificently and 308 took part throughout the 1980/81 season. 53 were members of the Pike Anglers Club, 59 were 'unattached' to any particular club, but the great majority, 196, were members of the Fenland Association of Anglers, the umbrella association for the Fenland angling clubs. I was responsible for organising the cull and collecting the results, which was done by ringing all the anglers involved every fortnight and noting details. This was supplemented by daily checks on the bank by our bailiffs, who reported who was where and what was being caught. This also allowed me to weed out any reports that seemed unreliable; for example, if an angler claimed to be fishing a certain water, but had not been seen regularly be bailiffs, his reports were discounted.

The final cull returns for 1980/81 show that 1,447 pike, weighing 6,540 lb, and 984 zander, weighing 3,110 lb had been removed, and that the original targets had been exceeded. The tables show the full story.

The successful completion of the cull meant that the second part of the operation could then start. A massive re-stocking of the system with bream and roach began at once, to reduce the predator prey relationship. All the fish stocked were over 6 inches in length, to ensure that they would not be devoured by the zander, and in the hope that they would spawn successfully. In addition, regular surveys of fish populations, using fast improving methods, continue to the present day. I left the fisheries service in 1983 and am grateful to Pat Noble, Martin Stark and John Adams for the up-to-date details of survey reports.

The reports indicate a much better predator/prey balance. For example, in 1985 the Middle Level Main Drain showed a 13 per cent biomass of predators compared with 50 per cent five years earlier. New techniques of marking fish and monitoring their movements throughout

Cull by rod and line of pike and zander from the Middle Level system of drains, 16 June 1980 to 14 March 1981

1. Reports received

	PIKE		ZANDER	
Source	*No.*	*Weight (Kg)*	*No.*	*Weight (Kg)*
Fenland A.A. members (196)	769	1427	407	532
Pike A.C. members (53)	421	886	441	643
Unattached anglers (59)	257	658	136	240

2. Details of cull

	PIKE		ZANDER	
WATER	*No.*	*Weight (Kg)*	*No.*	*Weight (Kg)*
Middle Level Main Drain	132	351	226	398
Pophams Eau	74	180	107	182
Sixteen Foot Drain	209	461	150	243
Twenty Foot River	353	822	244	291
Forty Foot Drain	151	234	42	48
Bevills Leam	99	205	66	79
Old course of River Nene	266	447	75	122
Yaxley Lode/Black Ham/ N.W. Cut	28	49	17	3
Whittlesey Dyke	135	222	57	49
Totals	1447	2971	984	1415
Cull target		2478		639
Additional zander culled		493		776

the system have also been perfected. These have shown some staggering results: roach put into the Relief Channel moving very quickly out into the Fenland system of waterways. These fish were part of a massive re-stocking of the channel. Over fifteen tons of fish were put in, and the Fisheries Section are hopeful that angling prospects will improve.

I no longer fish the Fen waters in the way I used to. Like many anglers I found pastures new when the fishing declined. Like me they have tended to avoid fishing the Fens, and that may be a mistake. It would be unfair of me to point to definite conclusions, but my experiences in the Fens have left an indelible mark, and I feel that a little analysis coupled with some crystal-ball gazing would not go amiss.

I now feel that the re-stocking of the Relief Channel in the early 1960s was an act of great significance. Firstly I am sure that many roach and bream moved out of the channel into the adjacent Fenland drains. The recent marking and recorded movements of fish lends weight to this theory, as does the zander migration. In the 1970s we did not fully realise just how mobile fish were, and what I think happened was this. In the 1960s the Fenland waters were probably overstocked with the offspring of the re-stocked fish, which resulted in the tremendous catches and, more significantly, in a boom time for predators. Throw into this melting pot a new predator whose spread and whose effect on other fish we could only guess at, and we have a recipe for disaster.

With hindsight there has been vociferous criticism of the zander cull and it is easy to forget just how desperate the situation was in 1980. It is all rather like voicing a 1987 opinion that Britain would win the war; in 1941 there would have been a lot less support for the idea. What the cull did was unite anglers and the Water Authority in the largest fishery management operation ever carried out in Great Britain. It was positive direct action against a serious problem, and it worked.

But what of the future? The drains have not yet produced the superb catches of the 1960s and early 1970s. Perhaps these results were artificial, produced by the massive restocking of 1960, and perhaps what we have now is the norm. If so it is interesting to remember the 1985/86 Relief Channel re-stocking with fifteen tons of fish. Perhaps we have set the whole cycle in motion yet again, only this time we have not put in any zander. They are already present.

The Mountain Lakes of Cumbria

MALCOLM BANNISTER

The English Lake District lies within the modern county of Cumbria in north-west England. It covers an area of about 800 square miles and is centred on the romantic lakeside village of Grasmere where the famous poet William Wordsworth lies buried.

It is an unusually inspiring place to fish for pike, not least because the whole area is dominated by rugged mountains. Scafell Pike, at 3,206 feet, is the highest of a series of mountains which tower against the skyline and plunge dramatically down into numerous large lakes.

Most of the lakes contain pike up to and above the twenty pound mark but the sheer scale of the waters available makes it difficult for the newcomer to know where to start. Indeed there are so many opportunities for the visitor that one would need to fish for a whole lifetime to achieve realistic results on most waters.

It is because of this that I made the decision eight years ago to concentrate my efforts on one particular water. I still make short trips to other lakes, but I believe that on such large waters better results can be obtained by spending a lot of time on one particular water, rather than trying to fish them all. The lake I fish shall remain nameless but it nestles in the shadow of mighty Skiddaw and is typical in many ways of the large freshwater lakes in this area.

It seems fair to say that these mountain lakes have been somewhat overlooked by modern pike anglers, perhaps because they lack the reputation for producing fish in the 30 lb to 40 lb class. However, fish up to around 35 lb have been reported from these lakes, and now that perch populations seem to be increasing the chances of more very big pike seem better each year. I certainly hope that one of these super fish come to my bait in the not too distant future!

It is surprising how many visitors to the Lake District expect the pike in these large waters to behave like those from large reservoirs. Such anglers normally expect the Lakes to fish well in winter, but poorly in summer. However, in my experience the exact opposite is the case. Over several years I have noticed that the pike become most active in June and July, slowing off a little in August and then feeding well again during the months of September and October. However, once the cold

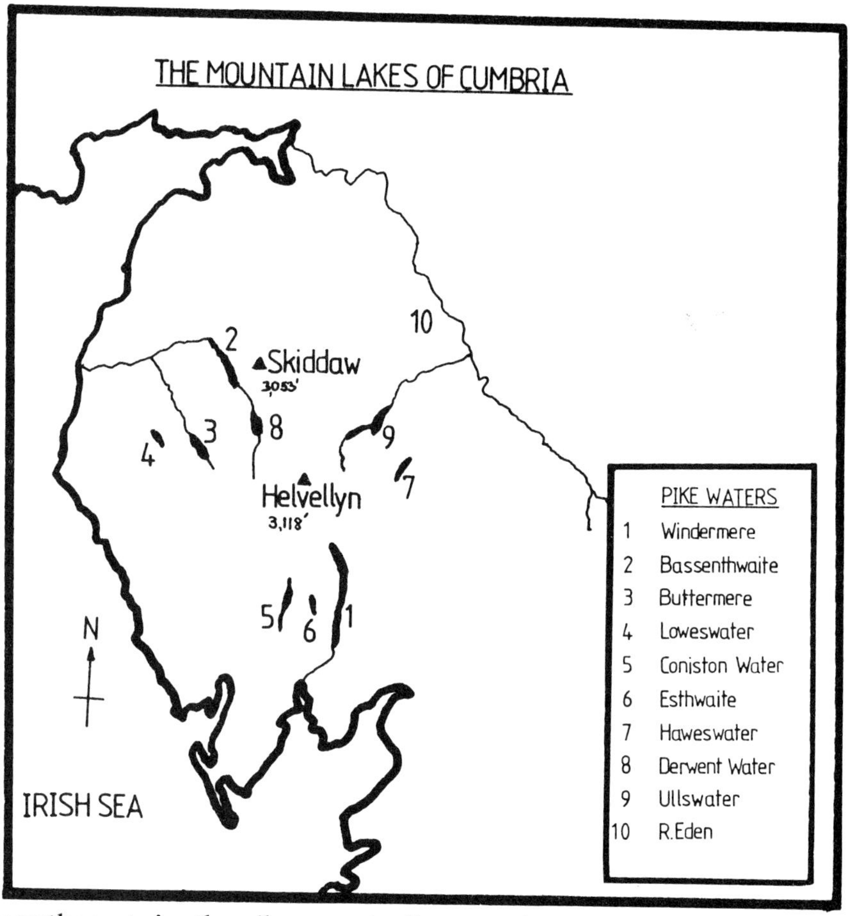

weather sets in, the pike seem to disappear for weeks on end. In reality I think they just lay up in holding areas, only feeding when mild conditions prevail for two of three days.

Over the years I have come to the conclusion that Cumbrian lake pike exist in large numbers and move around a lot. Indeed after fishing in certain areas regularly over the years I have been amazed at how infrequently I make repeat captures. This is a very healthy sign in my opinion, not least because it is less likely to cause harm to the fish themselves. If catching the same fish turns you on, fair enough, but it's not for me, nor is fishing amongst the crowds. One of the real advantages of fishing the Cumbrian lakes is that you can leave the crowds behind.

At the time of writing 1 August 1987, I am making plans for my eighth trip to fish the lakeland waters of Cumbria since the season opened on 16 June. It may become a little busy with holiday makers at times, but this is more than compensated for by the fact that I am

Perfect stillness on a piker's dawn. (Photo: M. Bannister)

fishing amid some of the most picturesque scenery on this planet Earth.

Having stated that pike are most active throughout the warmer months the question of location must now be faced.

I have found that pike lie very close to the bank during June and July: in fact 20 lb plus fish have been caught in just four feet of water. These pike are actually feeding on the perch that have come into the shallows to mop up the minnows that are so abundant in the summer months. Having said that, I always try to keep an open mind, and have taken fish to just short of twenty pounds in over thirty feet of water, while anglers fishing the shallow bays and points (up to eight feet deep) have had relatively quiet days just taking a handful of jacks. The policy of keeping an open mind certainly paid off for two of my friends. On the last day of the season, in just five feet of water, I netted a 22 lb pike for Dave and on the following 16 June (in the same swim) I netted a 20 lb 1 oz fish for Derek. So by all means fish shallow water (up to eight feet deep in the summer) and deep water in the winter, but don't be afraid to reverse the procedure; you never know, it might well produce the big fish you are seeking.

It seems to me that we used to have long hot summers, but for some unknown reason they now appear to be a thing of the past, but no matter what the weather, we still have around fifteen hours of daylight to contend with during the early part of the season. My records and experience tell me that dawn till midday and 7 pm till dark are the best

Malcolm Bannister finds perfect solitude amid the mountain lakes of Cumbria. (Photo: M. Bannister)

times to fish, so you will have to be up with the proverbial lark to catch the larger fish.

Recalling a recent trip when I arrived at the lake at 7 pm, up went the brolly camp and out went the usual three rods. By 9 pm I had four pike that weighed between eight and ten pounds. After a few hours sleep in the bivi I was fishing once again at 3.20 am. By 4 am I had netted a 13 lb pike taken on half mackerel and a 15 lb 12 oz pike on pat perch livebait. So if you are one for lying in bed in the morning you may well miss out on the better stamp of fish during the summer months.

During the winter months results can be very poor although big fish can still be caught from time to time. For some reason morning sessions seem more favourable in winter but are far less productive in my experience than during summer. In winter the secret to success lies in sheer single-minded persistence, and the will to fish on in the face of some of the most appalling conditions of cold and rain which can be found in Britain. Never forget that the weather can be particularly bad in Cumbria, sudden gales and squalls blow straight down from the mountains so it is important to dress accordingly.

Having covered the subject of location and feeding periods I shall

Malcolm Bannister holds a 20 lb 12 oz pike taken on the specialist techniques described in this chapter. (Photo: M. Bannister)

now deal with the important subject of methods. In my opinion the best method for Cumbria lake pike is the standard float paternostered livebait. In fact, livebaits on this rig out-fish deadbaits by about ten to one. When paternostering or ledgering live or deadbaits a weak lead link is essential. The lakes are full of snaggy rocks and boulders and if you fail to use a weak link (of about 6 lb b.s.) then a good fish could easily be lost when the arseley bomb becomes snagged up.

Whilst on the subject of paternostered baits, I have been using a ten-foot paternoster length when fishing in the deep water and confronted by a steep drop off. You obviously can't cast too well with such a long rig. However, I coil the ten-foot 'tail' up and tie it with PVA string. This method of fishing livebaits has been most successful for me and has led me to catch several fish upwards of 20 lb. It is not easy to say for certain why this rig works so well but I suggest it is by virtue of increased bait visibility in deep water. The standard three-foot rig would present baits below the field of vision and hence runs would be confined to deep-swimming fish. However, the ten-foot rig (as shown in the diagram) presents a livebait in full view of any marauding pike, and this probably explains why it is such a successful method.

The use of foreign livebaits such as roach and carp is not recommended because they are not natural species for the waters, although

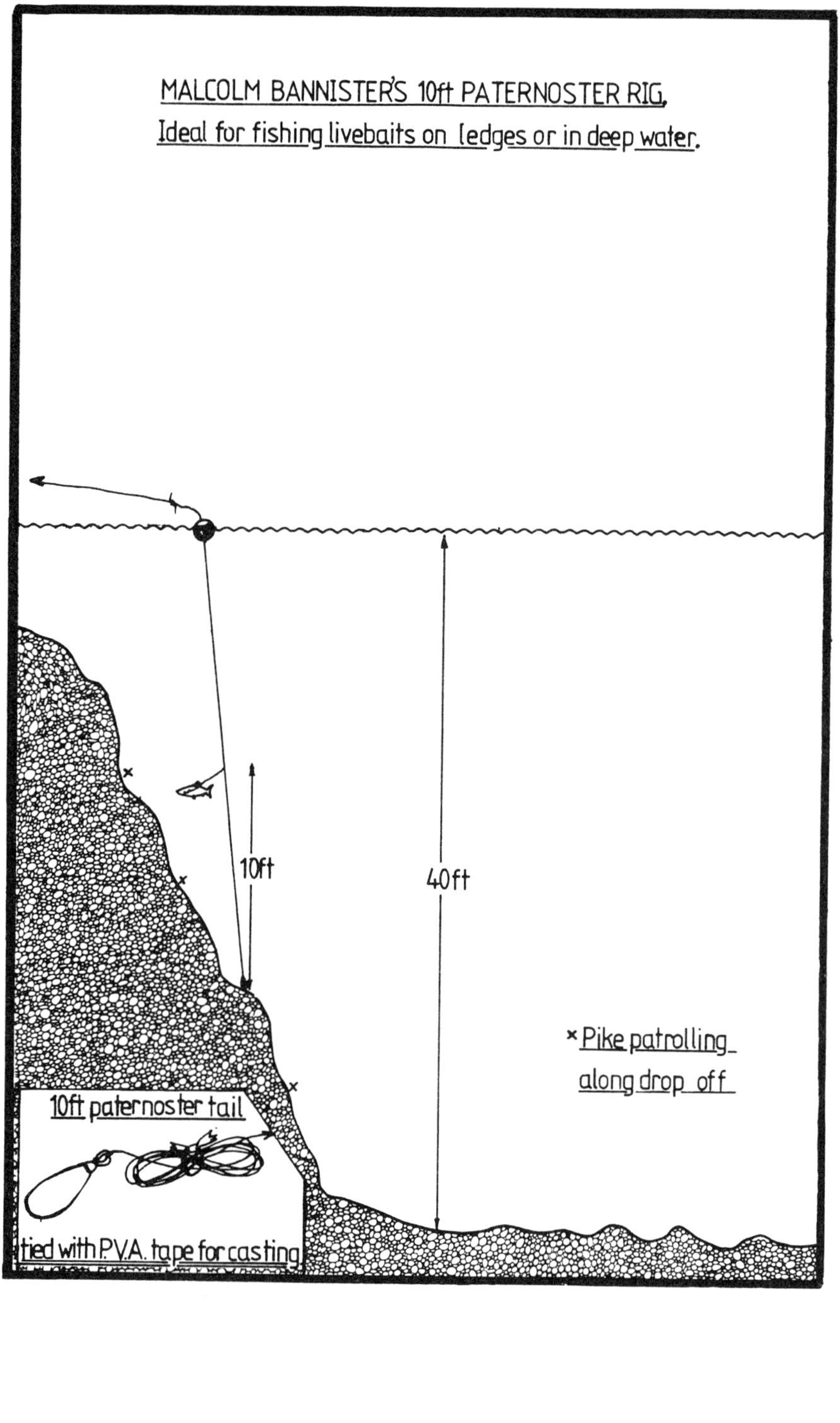

MALCOLM BANNISTER'S 10ft PATERNOSTER RIG.
Ideal for fishing livebaits on ledges or in deep water.
10ft
40ft
× Pike patrolling along drop off
10ft paternoster tail
tied with P.V.A. tape for casting

they are in fact widely used by visiting pike anglers and I have had reports of them being caught by anglers fishing for perch and trout.

Deadbaits are slow but cause no problems except when using seabaits: the eels can fillet a bait off the hooks in minutes and are a real nuisance in the summer. The best deadbaits are mackerel, trout, perch and eel section, which all account for some very good fish. I recently had a run on an eel section which was dropped after taking a few feet of line. I waited a minute or so before reeling in fairly quickly to avoid snagging up. I had just stopped reeling and lifted the bait out of the water when a large pike came 'flying' out of the water in a determined effort to steal my bait; so be warned – the Lakeland pike love eel section. The use of deadbaits can be slow but the weight of the pike caught is usually high compared to livebaits, which give a higher proportion of smaller pike.

One final word on Lakeland pike caught in summer: you really have to lean into the fish, for they fight like tigers. Pike don't take well to being out of the water for too long in the summer and you may well find you have to hold them level in the water for several minutes before they recover enough to be allowed to swim away.

I hope I have whetted your appetite for Lakeland pike. If you do decide to pay a visit, please respect the National Park and leave no litter in this most beautiful and tranquil of settings. After all we don't want anglers getting a bad name as this could lead to the loss of some of the finest pike angling in the country.

Enquiries on Lakeland fishing to:

Lake District Special Planning Board
National Park Office
Brockhole
Windermere

Tel. Windermere 6601

Yorkshire River Pike

BILL WINSHIP

It was over twenty years ago that I first became interested in pike fishing and like many other young anglers of the sixties I was inspired by people like Dennis Pye, Peter Hancock and a host of other fishermen who made impressive catches of big pike. In those far off days I was staggered at the huge size of those Norfolk pike shown weekly in press reports, and I found it difficult to understand why such fish were seldom reported from my home county of Yorkshire.

Now, with twenty years hindsight, I realise there are a number of reasons for this. Firstly, Yorkshire lacks the large still waters required to produce Norfolk-sized pike. Secondly, a large area of Yorkshire is dominated by high moorlands unsuited to pike; whilst good fishing waters do exist on the lowlands, they are mostly orientated to game and match fishing, and a lot of the pike get killed.

However, whilst the Yorkshire rivers seem to lack large numbers of press-worthy 'twenties' they are well populated with smaller fish weighing up to around 19 lb. Such fish are well distributed throughout all but the most polluted rivers. This situation makes it impossible for the Yorkshire angler to compete on equal terms with anglers on the big fish waters of Norfolk and Cambridgeshire, yet in terms of scenic quality and hard-fighting pike the Yorkshire rivers are in a class of their own and in many ways better than anywhere else in England.

Most of the Yorkshire rivers flow through landscapes ranging from the steep-sided glacial valleys of the Pennine moorlands down to the low and flat Vale of York. Pike thrive in all these varied conditions and provide the angler with a whole range of opportunities seldom found in other parts of the country. This chapter contrasts pike fishing in the fast river situation with pike fishing on the lowland plain. It is an angler's study of contrast, not only about the changing conditions found in the rivers, but also about how these changes affect the pike and our sporting prospects.

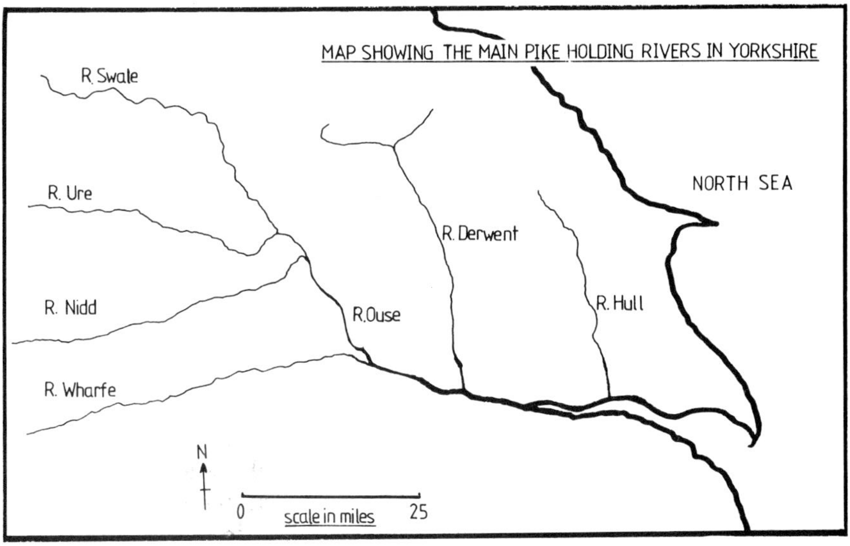

FAST-RIVER PIKE

When one consider that most of the Yorkshire rivers are fed by streams which rise above the 2,000-foot contour it is hardly surprising that they are cold and fast flowing in nature. These waters spring from the Yorkshire moorlands which experience cold, and even sub-arctic, conditions. Trees and shrubs are stunted, farming is restricted to rough grazing and the rivers can only support a small head of trout. Pike are seldom found in these highland areas, but as the rivers descend towards the 500 foot contour, pike numbers begin to increase. Of course, these fast river sections do not produce many big pike, but 15–20 lb fish do turn up from time to time, and the experience of catching pike at all in such unusual circumstances is a joy in itself.

The Yorkshire rivers which offer these conditions include the Ure, Swale, Nidd, Wharfe, Rye and a multitude of small streams which together provide hundreds of miles of water. Most of these rivers are avoided by modern pike anglers because they fail to produce the twenty-pound fish which are so popular these days. However, the peace and solitude afforded by these rivers can compensate for the lack of big fish. Success on such waters is not measured in pounds and ounces, but rather in the sheer pleasure of catching pike in such wonderful surroundings. Fast river pike are very sporting fish too; although they tend to be fairly small and streamlined they fight harder, pound for pound, than any other pike I have yet caught. They are tenacious, well toned, solid fish which seem generally more athletic than still water pike. For many years I have nursed the theory that fast river pike have

LONGDITUDINAL CROSS SECTION OF THE YORKSHIRE RIVERS (based on Ure and Ouse)

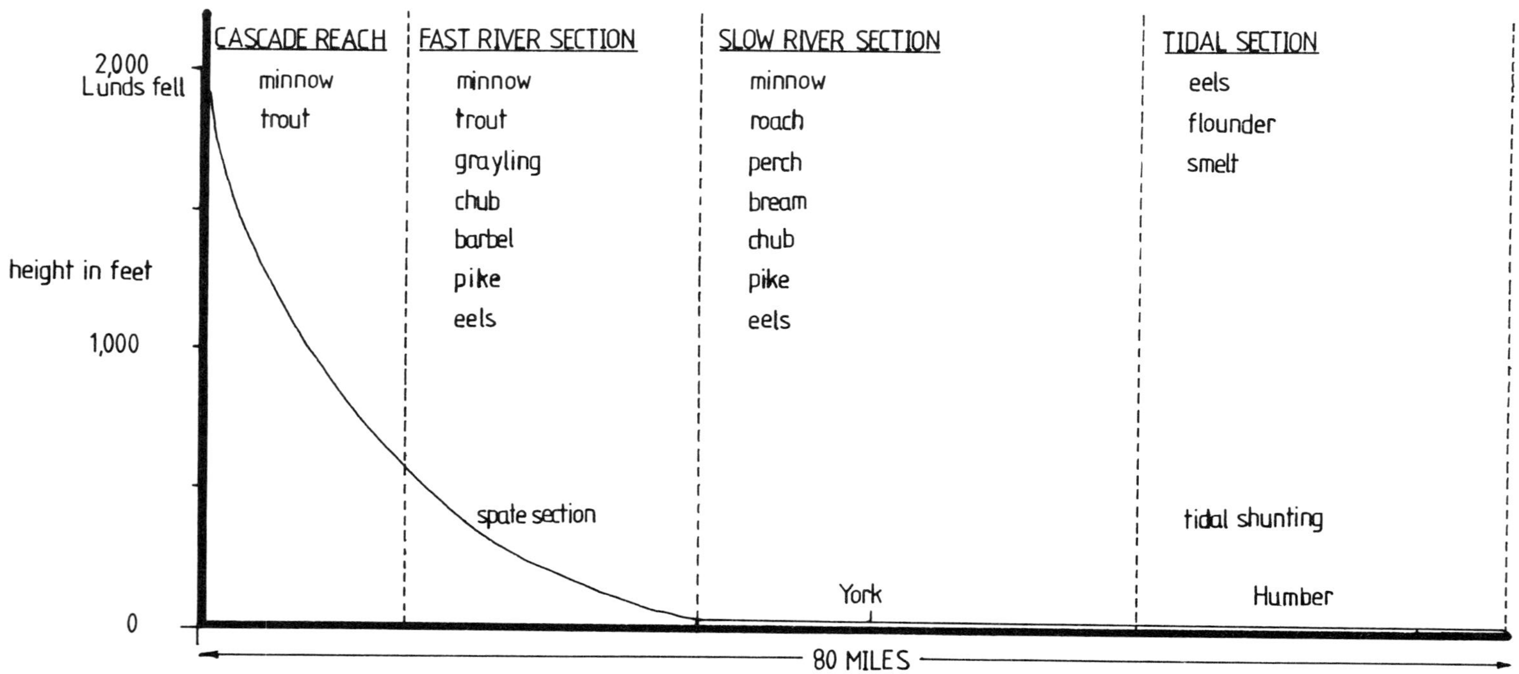

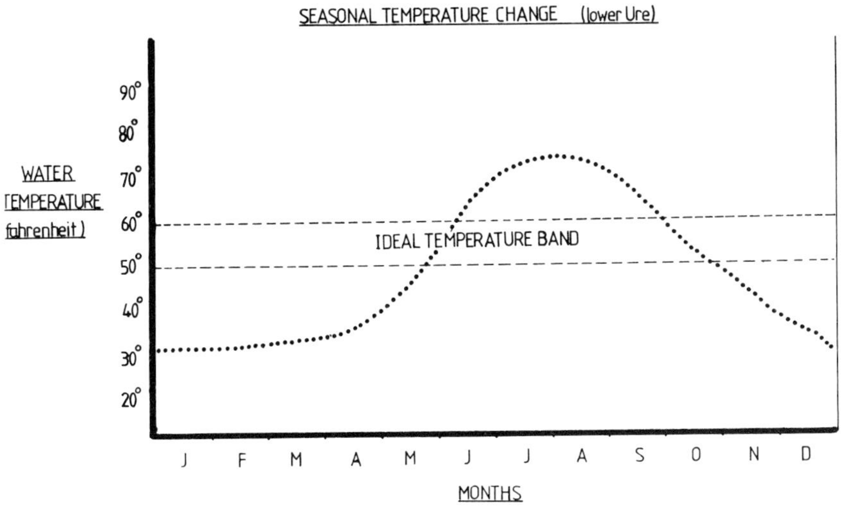

TEMPERATURE GRAPH For many years I have noticed that river pike seem to feed best when water temperatures hover between 50–60 degrees fahrenheit. These temperatures often come in May and September which I have found best on the fast Yorkshire rivers.

a higher metabolic rate than lake pike to help them cope with their generally more inhospitable habitat. Such a theory could explain why the fast water pike in Yorkshire fail to reach the size their cousins attain in the lower reaches (discussed in the following section).

The fact remains, though, that most northern spate rivers are temperamental and can change dramatically from day to day. Within hours sudden changes in air temperature can be transmitted through rainwater into the whole river system . Such fast changes seem to have an adverse effect on the feeding habits of most freshwater fish and sport can suffer badly. The worst effects are felt in October when the first freezing winter showers fall on the high Pennines. Such conditions seem to cause the pike to simply disappear for weeks on end. It is my belief that these temperature changes effectively 'shock' the fish so much that they are unable to feed, until, of course, they finally adjust to their new conditions. This may partly explain why these river pike are such unpredictable feeders, and why they can seemingly vanish for weeks on end. The diagram above shows the annual temperature changes on the upper Ure. The readings are based on measurements taken over several years.

Although feeding periods tend to be sporadic, pike location is easy to read on these rivers. Waters like the Swale, Ure and Nidd tend to flow in a series of fast glides and rapids which are broken by intermittent pools of slow deep water. Sometimes the rapids will flow for two or

What fast-river pike lack in size is made up for in their numbers. Here Bill Winship holds a brace of low doubles from the Yorkshire Ure. (Photo: Bill Winship)

three miles but wherever these swift waters suddenly run into a deep pool for four or five hundred yards, there is a good chance that pike will be there. Once located, these holding areas can provide good sport all the year round, but they are fragile, and if they are over fished then the pike can move elsewhere, so it pays to keep the exact whereabouts of these places a secret. Such hotspots can often go unnoticed for years at a time, mainly because pike anglers fail to recognise that the area holds pike at all. One such place has afforded me sport for over twenty years and is as good for pike fishing now as it was in the mid-sixties – and I have yet to see another pike angler fishing it.

In summer the pike tend to move out of the deep areas into the

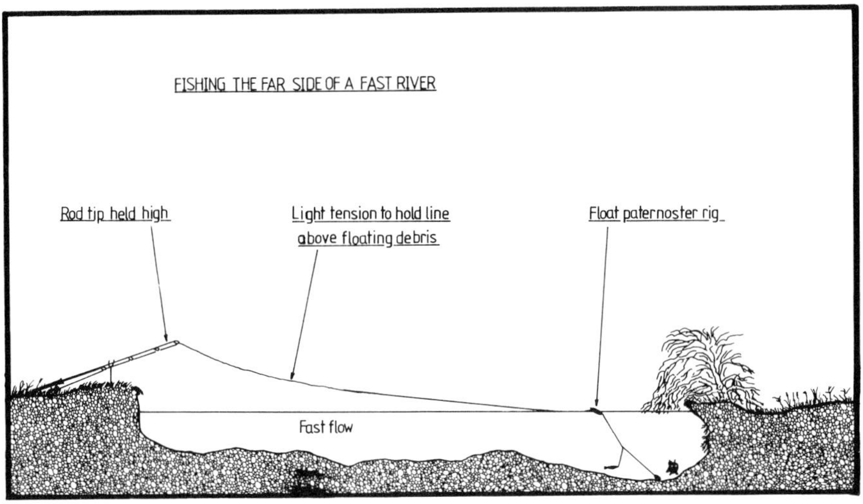
FISHING THE FAR SIDE OF A FAST RIVER
Rod tip held high
Light tension to hold line
above floating debris
Float paternoster rig
Fast flow

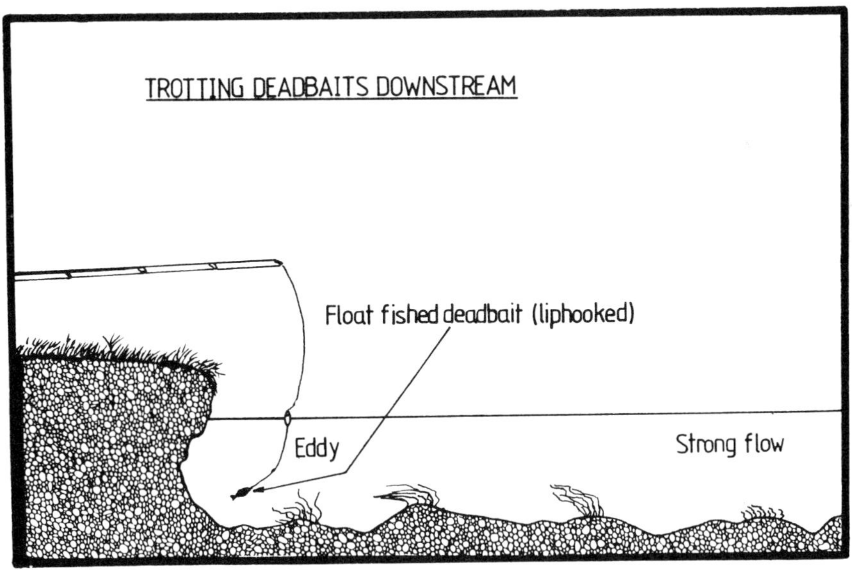
TROTTING DEADBAITS DOWNSTREAM
Float fished deadbait (liphooked)
Eddy
Strong flow

adjacent areas of shallow water (both up and downstream of the deeps) and provide good sport on spinning tackle. Floating plugs and deadbaits worked along the margins can be deadly for catching summer pike. Livebaits are also good, but these need to be tethered on paternoster rigs to prevent them from running into the weed-beds and snags. My favourite method is to cast a paternostered livebait under overhanging willows at the opposite bank. Such areas are rarely fished, and invariably hold a few pike. This special technique requires a large float and a 2 oz lead to anchor the rig, as shown in the diagram.

For searching out unknown stretches of river it pays to be mobile and for this kind of work the trotted deadbait is unbeatable. This method is very simple and involves allowing a deadbait to drift downstream past marginal weed-beds. Once the bait has drifted into the required position it can be drawn back along the riverside in a slow enticing manner. The rate of retrieve should be varied according to the season. F. J. Taylor once commented that half a turn of the reel handle every thirty seconds is fast enough and I would agree with this, in cold conditions. However, during June with fast rising water temperatures I would set the rate of retrieve at about one turn of the handle every five or ten seconds. This would be slow enough to attract a big pike yet fast enough to cover a large area of river bank throughout the day.

It has often been said, but it bears repeating, that fast river pike are usually found to lie within about seven feet of the bankside and this is why trotted deadbaiting (along the side of the river) is such a useful method. Livebaits can be used but they tend to swim into the side and soon die from repeated casting. Deadbaits provide the answer to trotting on rivers because they are easy to manipulate, especially when used in conjunction with a long purpose-built river rod. I use a 14-foot-long glass fibre rod which is invaluable for trotting deadbaits downstream past marginal weed-beds. The extra length is also useful for passing the line over the top of tall bushes as one moves downstream. This is useful when fishing long stretches of water as it saves having to recast the bait and cause unnecessary disturbance along the fishing area. A long rod is also helpful when fishing in snag-ridden water. The extra length provides greater control over a big fish and allows the angler to exert pressure in the right direction. Many of the fast-river hotspots I fish are full of snags and it is in these places that the long rod comes into its own.

One of the most common snags on the Yorkshire rivers are the sunken logs which steadfastly cling to the river bed. These obstacles are often quite immovable and represent a threat to both tackle and fish. However, with a long rod and strong tackle it is possible to bully even big pike up to the surface out of harm's way. Great care needs to be taken with knots as these often constitute the weakest link between man and fish; the line should be at least 15 lb bs. Sadly though, with the best will

Bill Winship struggles to hold onto an 18 lb fast-river pike. The four-foot-high pile of drift wood behind the author was the result of a forty-eight-hour flash flood and shows just how changeable northern spate rivers can be. (Photo: B. Winship)

in the world good pike will invariably be lost in these conditions as pike sometimes snag themselves before the strike. It is for this reason that I take the extra precaution of using single hooks because I believe that they will do less harm if left in the pike's mouth.

I became a firm single hook advocate after a 20 lb river pike broke my tackle on some unseen snags of which I was unaware. Half-an-hour later the same fish accepted a second bait and was duly landed, and I was able to remove the single hook which it had snapped off earlier. I don't believe I would have taken that fish a second time if I had been using the standard snap tackle rig; that is why I now use the single hook rigs most of the time.

Whichever rigs and tackles are used, great care needs to be taken with these river pike because their numbers are already greatly reduced by match and game anglers who see the pike as a threat in these rivers. Yorkshire game anglers still nurse a blood lust for the pike and in this area the message of the Pike Anglers' Club seems to have fallen on deaf ears. In fact, as game anglers seem to put great store in the idea of 'catching for the table' the division, or lack of understanding, between pike and trout men seems to be as wide as ever.

THE YORKSHIRE OUSE. SLOW-RIVER PIKE

Fast rivers like the Swale, Ure, Nidd and Wharfe gradually deepen and become more sluggish as they enter the Vale of York. It is here that most of the Yorkshire rivers come together to form one great river called the Yorkshire Ouse. The Ouse is a fairly typical lowland river in that it meanders mile after mile through rich arable farmlands. Its width varies between forty and seventy yards and it supports vast weed beds which are full of small fish.

These conditions provide the ideal habitat for pike and the richness of the surroundings is very much reflected in the size and condition of the pike which inhabit this water. Over the years I have made a study of Yorkshire river pike and I have found that in the river Ouse the pike grow to a maximum weight of about 30 lb compared with a maximum weight of about 19 lb in the shallow and fast waters discussed in the previous section. However, its not just the weight of these river pike that increases downstream; they also become fatter. The following diagram illustrates this phenomenon and shows how the richness of the habitat is reflected in the condition of the pike.

The sheer quality and size of the pike in this part of the river make it a very attractive water for the pike angler. However, despite its potential, the Ouse presents the newcomer with a formidable challenge. It is a vast water covering thousands of acres. Some of the best pike fishing areas are easy to find, occuring in the classic holding areas, like weir pools, lock gates and large bends. But these places do not necessarily hold pike all the year round and the art of catching them lies in knowing both when and where to find them. The situation is further complicated by the fact that many of the best pike can be taken from some of the most unlikely areas. For example, in the river section which flows through the centre of York several 30 lb pike have been reported, including the Yorkshire Ouse record caught by Mr Lee Maloney, a fish which weighed over 31 lb. There are many lock cuttings on the Ouse which at first appear to provide the ideal harbour for pike, but in my experience they only hold good fish in the period between January and late February. This is the time when large numbers of pike start to congregate in readiness for spawning. Weir pools are often a safe bet but can be particularly good in summer when large numbers of fry collect around the plunge pool in the well oxygenated water. In winter however the pike avoid the weirs as floodwaters make them dangerous and uninhabitable. The Ouse is frequently flooded out in winter but this should not deter the angler as the river fishes well even when it carries ten feet of flood water. Most river anglers seem to be deterred by the prospect of a flooded river but in my experience floodwaters create a whole range of opportunities not available when the river is in trim. Indeed under floodwater conditions

Lee Maloney holds his 31 lb Yorkshire Ouse pike. This is thought to be the largest fish to have been taken from the river, though much bigger pike are believed to inhabit the system. This fish had a huge girth of twenty-five and a half inches, and is typical of the well conditioned fish which thrive in this lower section of the Ouse system. (Photo: L. Maloney)

YORKSHIRE RIVER PIKE — contrast between fast and slow river conditions

RIVER SECTION	FOOD FISH	HABITAT	weight ceiling	age at 20lb	SEASON	SHAPE
Fast river section as found on river Swale, Ure or Nidd	minnow, dace, brown trout, chub and grayling	The fast river section is occupied by fast moving, mobile fish species. In order to survive the pike take on a streamlined shape and are generally small and athletic, this helps them thrive in fast flowing water.	20lb	12year	summer	
					spring	
Slow reaches of the lower ure and ouse	perch roach bream eels and flounder	The slow flowing river ouse is shallow weedy and rich in fry fish. In these surroundings the pike feed well without expending much effort, as a result some of the pike grow very large.	30lb	12year	summer	
					spring	

the pike are bullied by the current into areas of easily recognised slack water. They also feed well and often congregate in large numbers. Because the water is coloured you can get very close to your quarry without spooking. This is almost impossible in clear water conditions.

In Yorkshire the season opens on 1 June and at this time the pike are often found in the shallow streamy runs where they love to bask in the early summer sun. I have taken pike up to 22 lb in marginal weed beds standing in only two feet of water. These fish will take either live or deadbaits but great stealth is required to take fish from shallow clear water and it is often best to fish just before dusk or dawn when light conditions provide a certain amount of cover. As the season progresses heatwaves tend to drive the pike into the deep water sections where they hide from the sun. This is the time when the pike seem to stop feeding for weeks on end, but the deadlock can often be broken by floods which bring fresh water and seem to get the fish feeding again. This is another example of floodwaters bringing opportunities to the pike angler, but you have to know about them before you can benefit.

During prolonged periods of very cold weather the flow conditions often fall to their summer levels and the water can become very clear. It is rare that the river actually freezes over but good fish can still be taken, even in the coldest of conditions. At such times I have often found pike in the middle of the river in deep water. Deadbaits fished just off the bottom can score well in very cold weather but I prefer paternostered livebaits fished in the deep central areas, or above weirs where fodder shoals tend to collect. I prefer to use a fairly long paternoster tail, up to about four feet long as this provides the bait with a wide area in which to work. Alternatively, buoyant deadbaits fished off the bottom can create similar effects. These buoyant baits are very attractive to river pike because the gentle current ensures that they move and sway about from side to side. I am sure the pike must realise the baits are dead when they take them but they do nevertheless seem to find the movement attractive.

My favourite deadbaits for this kind of fishing are the joey, or horse mackeral. The good thing about these baits is that they have very large mouths. This enables one to simply fill them up with chunks of old cork or any other buoyant material. I have tried injecting air into these fish to make them buoyant but the pressure of the deep water soon squeezes out the air bubbles, causing the bait to sink. If you use cork, however, the opposite occurs. As the pressure of the water increases so the cork inserts are held in place even firmer. For this kind of buoyant ledger rig it is possible to dispense with the float, but this often leads to lost tackle. As mentioned earlier, most of the best pike lies are festooned with snags and a straight ledgered deadbait trundling along the river bed soon finds them. A float, however, will hold the line above the snags and saves losing a lot of tackle, not to mention pike.

YORKSHIRE RIVER PIKE   from upland stream to lowland river

RIVER SECTION	SIZE POTENTIAL (approx)	BRIEF DESCRIPTION OF WATER
SMALL STREAM SECTION	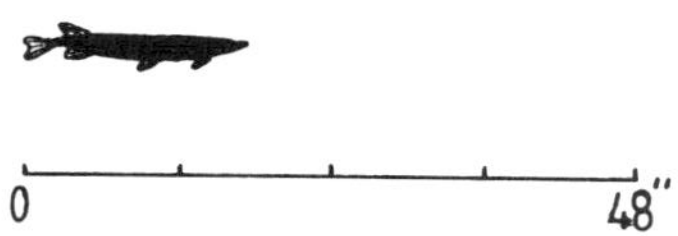	Small fast flowing trout streams seldom produce big pike in Yorkshire but they can provide sport with fish up to around the 5lb mark.
FAST RIVER SECTION	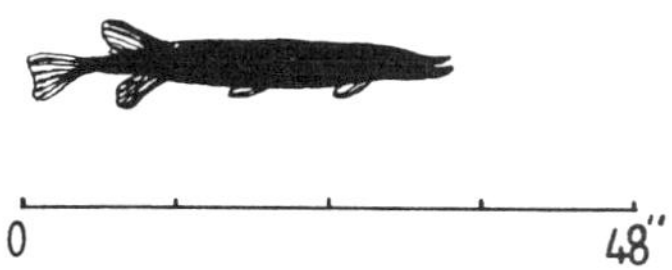	Fast rivers like the Swale, Ure and Nidd offer the chance of pike in the 10 - 20lb class.
SLOW RIVER SECTION	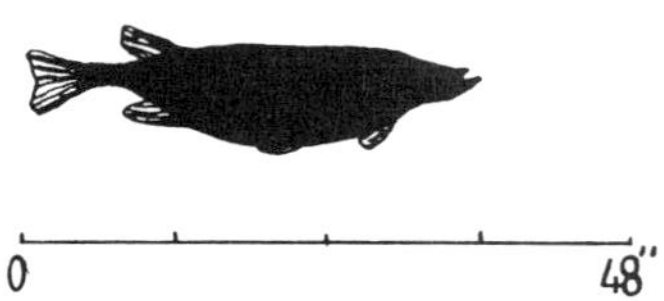	The slow fertile river Ouse supports shoals of bream roach and perch, pike have been taken up to a weight of 30lb in this river.

On rivers I tend to have a lot of faith in bait additives and attractants. These can be injected into the bait or simply smeared onto it. I prefer the latter as it is less wasteful and much easier to apply. It is not difficult to imagine how scent trails are carried downstream in rivers, and this surely makes them particularly helpful to the river angler. It is impossible to know how far pike will travel upstream to check any interesting scent trails but I would not be surprised if they came from four to five hundred yards' range. This may seem a long way, but it would only take a few minutes for water-borne substances to travel this far, and perhaps even less time for a hungry pike to respond. Of course the same kind of logic applies to the use of fish particles which can be used as 'groundbait'. With this kind of attractant it is best to feed the swim on a 'little and often' basis rather than simply fill the swim as soon as you arrive. Fish fragments soaked in commercial 'pike attractor' solution will thus keep those important scent trails travelling downstream all day long, thus increasing the chances of drawing a pike upstream. These methods take some of the emphasis away from having to find the 'right' place to fish. In fact it is possible to actually create the right place or hotspot, by regularly baiting up an area. This has the added benefit of making your pike grow bigger and fatter which can only improve results.

In the lower section of the Yorkshire Ouse system the river becomes tidal and suffers from the scourge of pollution. The shape and configuration of the lower river course makes it subject to 'tidal shunting' which helps to create a permanent barrier of pollution between the river and sea. As polluted water enters the Ouse via the river Aire and Calder it is shunted up and down the estuary for several weeks before it is finally released into the sea. This situation exaggerates the effects of pollution in the Ouse and prevents the seasonal migration of the salmon which were once so prolific in the county.

It is interesting to consider the effects that a large-scale re-introduction of salmon would have on the size and growth rates of Yorkshire river pike. Presumably such an influx of migratory fish would have a beneficial effect upon the size and number of pike in the system. However, my enquiries about the situation before the war, when salmon were still found in Yorkshire, have not supported this notion. Indeed, all the anglers I have spoken to who caught pike in the first half of the century in Yorkshire assure me that the pike fishing is as good, if not better, now than at any time within living memory. Sadly, if salmon did re-establish themselves in Yorkshire there could be dire consequences for pike interests. Such an occurrence would probably raise fishing rents beyond the reach of the coarse anglers who would be displaced by the salmon fraternity. This seems highly unlikely in the forseeable future though as recent efforts by the Yorkshire Water Authority to re-introduce salmon have failed.

Norfolk Pike

The Norfolk fisheries, collectively known as the Broads, are some of the most important coarse fisheries in England; why else would so many of our top anglers move house, home and job to be near to them, or travel hundreds of miles on weekend fishing trips. Make no mistake these shallow fertile waters are a coarse fisherman's paradise and are a great repository of specimen pike. This has been proven over the years by anglers like the late Jim Vincent, Pete Hancock, Derek Amies and a host of other anglers who have caught hundreds of big pike including seven over 35 lb in weight.

Against this background of legendary pike the Norfolk fisheries obviously deserve special treatment in any pike book. In order to help us understand these complex Norfolk waters Dan Leary has offered to share his thoughts on the subject. Dan has thirty-five years of angling experience in Norfolk backed by twenty-five years service as an official fisheries bailiff. He has taken many pike over 20 lb topped by a 39 lb 8 oz specimen. There can be few anglers who have equalled Dan's tally of Norfolk pike. Despite having caught what was almost certainly a new British record pike, Dan had never sought public recognition. Fortunately, in this chapter Dan has provided an illuminating insight into the habits and movements of Norfolk pike, based on his own experience of the Broads.

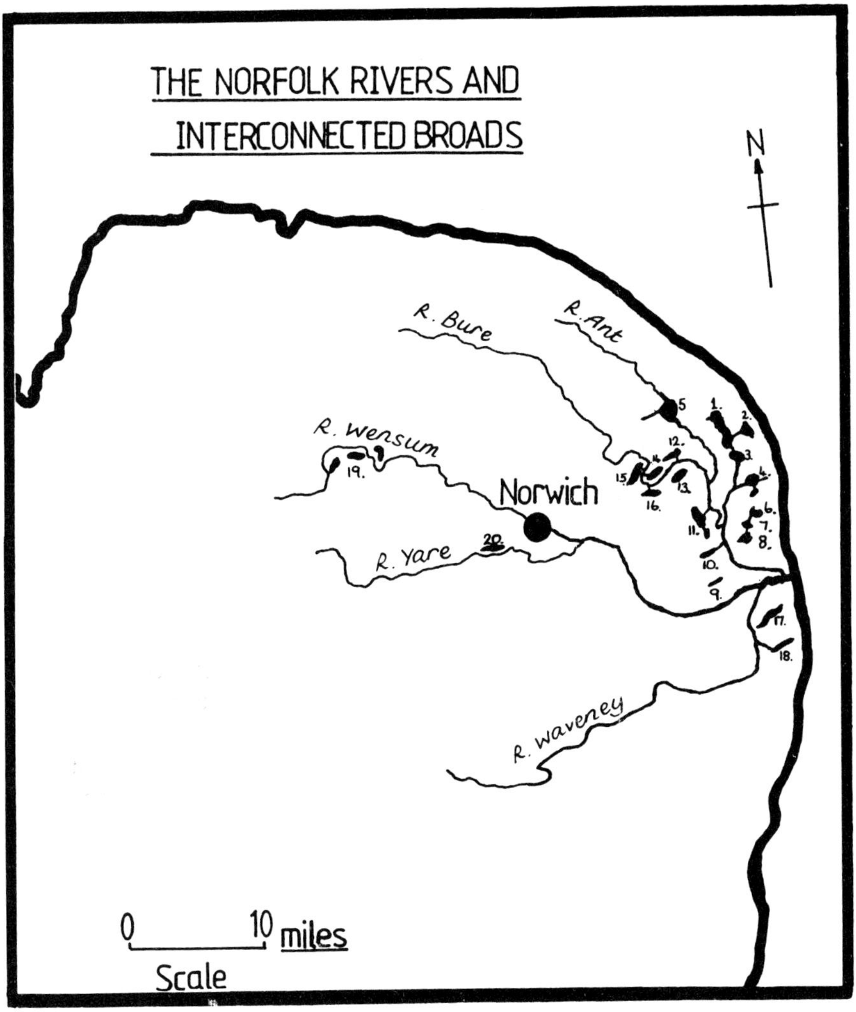

Key to Pike Waters

1	Hickling Broad	11	Ranworth Broad
2	Horsey Mere	12	Little Hoveton Broad
3	Heigham Sound	13	Decoy Broad
4	Martham Broad	14	Hoveton Gt. Broad.
5	Barton Broad	15	Wroxham Broad.
6	Ormesby Broad	16	Salthouse Broad
7	Rollesby Broad	17	Fritton Decoy
8	Filby Broad	18	Oulton Broad
9	Upton Broad	19	Lyng Pitts
10	South Walsham Broad	20	University Pond

Portrait of a pike angler. Dan Leary is a down to earth pike angler with enormous experience of fishing the Norfolk broads and rivers. His success as an angler is based on his close understanding of the waters he has fished for many years, rather than the use of high tech gear. Dan maintains that there is nothing really complicated about pike fishing but emphasises the importance of understanding the movements and feeding patterns of the pike. (Photo: D. Winship)

Fishing the Norfolk Broads

DAN LEARY

'Do a bit about piking in Norfolk' Bill said – so I started to tell him about the record pike I caught in December 1983. Record pike? Well yes, it must have been when I first landed it, for three hours later when it died and was weighed on attested scales it still went to 39 lb 8 oz. Pity it swallowed the hooks so deep – and still managed to eject the 12 oz herring, which in itself would have put my name up there right alongside Hancock and Amies. It made news at the time, but quickly faded into the background after a spate of record specimens from a Norfolk waterway called the Upper Thurne System. Nonetheless, it represented for me the culmination of a pike angling career stretching back over fifty-nine years. For the purpose of this articles, however, I start in 1960.

It was round about 1960 when places with romantic-sounding names were often written and talked about in the angling press. In particular, names like Hickling Broad, Heigham Sound, Horsea Mere, and homely names like Jim Vincent, Dennis Pye and others became regularly featured as having caught huge pike on those Norfolk waters.

At that time I was soldiering at Sandgate, Folkstone, and had only a couple of years left before qualifying for a pension. After completing my Regular Army career in 1961, I moved up to Norfolk.

By the time I had got the bungalow and garden in order it was the close season. Come June 16th I started to make the best of things. Having acquired a trailer, I loaded up the boat (an eleven-foot glass fibre job) and roach fishing gear and set off on the five minute run to Wroxham Broad.

In those days Wroxham Broad wasn't fished much except by casual holiday makers fishing from moored cruisers in the holiday season. Finding a quiet, reedy bay out of the main stream of traffic, I moored up in 10 feet of water, stuck on a maggot and started to catch roach. I would have preferred the shallows, but on arrival had seen a large cruiser go aground and cause a terrific disturbance. (Nobody thought of fishing for pike until October. My idea was to pass the time until then by testing the potential of Wroxham Broad as a readily available source of livebait for the real business planned for the autumn, on what is now usually referred to as the Upper Thurne System.) Probably the roach, too, liked the comparative quiet of the little bay. At the end of the morning I tipped back about three dozen roach to a pound, most of them around 3 lb 6 oz, just right for live or dead bait.

This is just one of several 30 lb pike which Dan Leary has taken from the Norfolk fisheries. Dan is now retired but still works as a water bailiff on a small lake near Lenwade in Norfolk. (Photo: D. Leary)

The weeks slipped by quite pleasantly. Occasionally a 3 lb tench or 4 lb bream would turn up to make things more interesting. One fine day a chap in a smart uniform hove to in his snappy little launch flying the Anglian Water pennant, introduced himself as the bailiff and asked to see my rod licence. After I had produced it we had a little chat. He too liked roach fishing and agreed that he also liked his job. Jokingly I told him, 'So would I'; in fact I'd put my name down. We both laughed, he switched on the ignition and quietly moved off down the broad and out of sight.

I never saw him again. He died a couple of months later. Shortly after our meeting he was struck with a terminal illness, I was to learn – an ex merchant navy captain who had never before had a day's illness. Subsequently I was to be interviewed by Anglian Water and in the face of severe competition was finally accepted as the ex captain's replacement. Such is life – and death. But to get back to fishing.

By early September and with only a few weeks to go I began to buy a few new items of pike tackle capable of standing up to the tough treatment expected on the Upper Thurne System. As things turned out, they were required even earlier than expected.

It wasn't a big tench I was playing on Wroxham Broad that particular September day, but at first it felt like it. It was a pike that had taken a roach that had taken my maggot, and I wasn't able to get it into my net. It didn't even give me the chance to try, but revealed its size before departing with my roach. About a yard long and 15 lb in weight I estimated. It got me thinking.

Before then I believed the Upper Thurne System had a monopoly of huge pike and not for one moment had I considered that anywhere else on the broads could produce such great pike sport. No harm in giving Wroxham Broad a trial I thought whilst waiting for October 1st.

As it happened, I stayed longer – much longer: not on Wroxham broad but almost exclusively within the Wroxham-Horning limits, and never regretted giving the Upper Thurne System a miss. In fact I stayed on Wroxham Broad rather too long that first time. Let me explain.

Nobody had told me of the mass migration of fish from many of the Broads in the autumn (usually October). There were lots of other things that I didn't know and had to find out the hard way. I started my lesson on Wroxham Broad and what I learned was to lead me ultimately to the elusive thirty.

But I wasted almost the whole of that first late autumn and winter flagging a barren water. Incidently, so did a few others. Perhaps, like me, they thought they were at fault, because weekly angling reports kept encouraging us with news like 'bags of pike to 20 lb caught on Wroxham Broad'.

Leaping ahead a decade or so from my first Broads (Wroxham) pike, I had in that time become quite an experienced and successful piker, having caught many pike over twenty. But I still had lots to learn and this is where old Jed the eel trapper came in. After an initial eyeball to eyeball confrontation when I wanted to inspect his nets, we began to understand each other and became good friends. He had a wealth of knowledge about fish and their habits; his living depended on it. I benefited from his knowledge. Consequently my learning period was that much shorter.

It was early October, the silly season was on the wane and I had time for a chat with Jed who was collecting up his nets down the Bure. He told me about this huge pike that had got into one of his nets and got stuck.

'Where was this?'

'Near the dyke entrance to the Decoy Broads.'

Dan with his record pike. This fish weighed well over the magical 40 lb mark when it was caught. Dan has never sought public recognition for this or any of the other huge pike he has caught over the years, and that is why he chose not to lodge an official claim. But those who have seen this pike are in no doubt about its record status! It is without doubt one of the largest pike ever taken in Britain. (Photo: D. Leary)

'How big was it?'

'Three inches longer than the transom of my boat here.'

'How long's that?'

'Fifty inches.'

'Fifty-three! Bloody Hell! Forty pound, would you say?'

'Oh, easy that. It was fat on my eels.'

'What did you do with it?'

'Put it back in the river alive. It was lucky I wasn't doing my lobster pots at the time.'

'Thanks Jed. I owe you a pint!'

No time was lost and for two consecutive days I flogged the area very thoroughly but without a sign of that pike, nor any other come to that. I thought it may have moved upstream for the coming winter, or even into the adjacent Decoy Broad, which I had fished before with excellent results throughout the season – a Broad which retained its fish all year round.

So I moved in again and took up where I left off, several sessions producing lots of doubles and two of twenty plus. On about the fifth visit, around noon I noticed storm clouds gathering over Crabbetts Marsh behind me and decided a move to lee was prudent. A couple of other piker, more prudent than I, said 'Cheerio' and rowed back towards the moorings and home.

Even as I rowed towards the shelter of tall trees on the west bank the wind got up and large drops of rain began to splash heavily on me. I should have turned and followed my friends, but didn't. I knew something big was brewing. By the time I got the anchors down fore and aft and the brolly up and secured (with difficulty) I was already damp and apprehensive. Within a few minutes I was downright bloody scared; it was the worst weather I'd fished in since having to sit out a blinding sandstorm on Lake Fimsha in the Suez Canal Zone.

I sat this one out too, peering at my two floats about fifteen yards away, riding the edge of the rough water which a little way further out resembled the Bay of Biscay at its worst. Dead ahead lay the safety of the sheltered moorings, now hidden from sight by the towering waves, the blinding spray and the early gathering gloom, but only about 150 yards away. But no way was I going to tackle the crossing voluntarily, I told myself; just sit it out as long as necessary.

By 3 pm it was quite dark. I was cold (partly through fear) and wet through with spray. The tall trees behind me creaked and groaned ominously in the gale-force westerly and old branches broke away and landed on the water with a resounding splash, too close for comfort.

Suddenly, almost directly behind me, there was a terrible crack that caused me to leap to my feet in terror. There and then I decided to leave *voluntarily*. I couldn't see which tree it was, but no sense in taking chances. Down with the brolly, up with the anchors and in with the baits, quickly – must put a bit of distance between me and those trees that threatened disaster.

In came one bait, no bother, as the boat bagan to slowly edge towards what awaited me. The other didn't; in fact, 'solid resistance', as they say. What a time to get a take. I could have done without it, particularly since this was no tiddler. The boat began to pick up speed under the increasing influence of the wind and the power of the pike, and the more I tried to put the brakes on the more determined the critter was to have its head.

We hit the first roller head on, changed up into top gear and we were riding the white horses at a fair rate of knots. Tally ho! I was in a pretty pickle, but it was spit or bust, and if I was going to go down I was going to go down fighting. It was in my favour that we were no more than perhaps 10 degrees off course from the moorings. Desperately I tried to steer that pike in the right direction – if it turned directly left or right I might have to cut the line immediately.

But it just kept going straight on, heading for a marshy and overgrown area where a safe landing was extremely dangerous and difficult in normal circumstances. Then, as disaster seemed imminent, I came to my senses, snapped off the reel check, picked up the oars and bent to the task. Slowly, very slowly, I made headway, gaining a little, losing a little, shipping a big wave every yard of the way to the moorings, just eight or so yards away but seeming like eight thousand.

At last I made it, completely exhausted but glad to be alive and in one piece – more or less. I rolled out of the boat and lay flat out on the sodden quay, in the pelting rain, for several minutes. Then I pulled myself together and after securing the boat picked up the rod and began to reel in. The pike was still on but, like me, had had enough; what little battle remained to be won was conducted around the moored boats, stepping precariously from one to the other.

Soon she was on the quay and what little light was left was sufficient to convince me that here was my first thirty. Not surprisingly, my torch wouldn't work. In any case, I don't think I would have had the strength to weigh it there and then even if it had worked – and, believe me, I badly wanted to get home as quickly as possible.

Round the corner in sheltered water was a large livebait box owned by two well known local pike anglers. What they will never know (unless they read this) is that one night a 32 lb pike kept their roach company in that box. I don't think it did them any harm.

Anyway, it was a lovely well proportioned fish with a length of 48 inches – the same as my 39 lb 8 oz, but 4 inches less in girth at 24 inches – and, all things considered, *the* most memorable. No, it wasn't the monster old Jed had told me about. As far as I know that was never caught and probably died of old age. But it has been seen at least once by me, I am convinced. Another memorable occasion.

Small to medium pike I lift out of the water by hand, and I was about to do this with a five pounder a few weeks later, near the spot that once harboured the thirty-two. Something 'a bit longer than Jed's transom' loomed up from nowhere and grabbed the little one across the body with jaws like a great white shark's. Another frightening experience on Decoy! This great lunker took off across the Broad at a steady lick whilst I paid off line, watching it carefully in the hope that any twitches would indicate the prey was being turned prior to swallowing. but it didn't happen and with just a few turns of line left on the reel, which held 200 yards, I stopped paying out, waited for the line to tighten and struck hard. As expected, all I got back was a badly mauled five pounder. The teeth marks indicated a pike with jaws at least an inch wider than the thirty-two's. I reckon I'd just missed my forty – not quite as thickset as my 39 lb 8 oz, but certainly several inches longer. With a little more luck or line that surely would have been my most memorable day.

The piker who recently told us in the local paper that 'blanks are frequent' and 'there's not may big pike left' (or little ones either) was not giving us the usual Upper Thurne System flannel. He was speaking the truth. Now how has this deplorable situation come about? I'll tell you.

Prymnesium has for years taken an increasing toll of all species of fish on the system, but particularly pike. Additionally, a number of big pike have been unofficially 'culled' and removed to other waters outside the area. The survivors, easy to locate immediately after an outbreak of prymnesium and eager to feed after an enforced fast, have been harried and hammered almost to the point of extinction. Few indeed are now left. Some will have managed to find sanctuary elsewhere.

Sorry to have to say it, but the future of the species on the Upper Thurne System looks bleak. In truth, the experts have become victims of their own success. But take heart. Don't go cancelling your Broads fishing holiday just yet. There is plenty of excellent sport to be had elsewhere if you know where to look, and you don't have to break the law to find it.

Location and a deep understanding of pike movements and feeding patterns have always been the key to success; never more so than on the Broads where, because of almost unique ecological factors, pike and other fish move more often, and further afield, and feed more unpredictably than in most other places. Knowledge of these habits and the correct application of that knowledge is of such importance that I feel compelled to go into some detail, at the expense perhaps of telling tales about what a clever chap I've been. Here we go.

If you hire a cruiser for your fishing holiday (useful with a dinghy in tow) a detailed two inch to a mile (1: 25,000) map of the broads is usually included. If not, get one at the Post Office or almost any stationer's. Also get yourself a local tide table, available at most tackle shops. Study them. Take them with you when you go for a pint at the riverside pub with stuffed fish on the wall. Even if they are inherited, it often means that the landlord is well informed, so talk to him when he is not busy. If he is, buy that scruffy looking chap covered in eel slime a pint; nobody knows more about fish movements and tides than one whose living depends on it.

Tide tables only tell you so much, by expanding on the local one. Briefly, there are two massive migrations of fish every autumn on the Broads, usually in October. Let's deal with the biggest first.

High tides mean salt. The higher tide the saltier it is, and the further up river it will penetrate. As most of the Broads are connected, they are almost all affected. Fish swim up river, ahead of the tide, until it peters out. Here they shoal up and feed and this is where you cash in – though perhaps not for long, because when the flood changes to ebb, the fish drop back with it, but only so far. With autumn comes higher (saltier) tides and shortly the lower reaches of the rivers Bure and Thurne become uninhabitable, (except, that is, to flounders, dabs and smelts) until the following spring.

In effect this means that as the season progresses and the tides gain strength the fish are forced further and further upstream and drop downstream less and less. Of course, there are stragglers, fish that don't conform to the norm, but I discovered that for the duration of the recognised Broads pike season, October to March, fishing below Horning and the Bure and Potter Heigham on the Thurne wasn't worth bothering about. Usually, the incoming tides (called floods) have little or no influence on the fish upstream of Horning Ferry with regard to salt, and even less influence half a mile further up at Horning Swan Bend (good moorings, good grub, often great fishing – what more do you want? – oh yes, good shops for 'er inboard').

Certainly the area between Horning and Wroxham is where I would choose to spend my pike fishing holiday, knowing what I do about the area's potential. Starting, say, at Horning you, like the fish, up-anchor and follow them perhaps as far as Wroxham (capital of the Broads) if the tides get troublesome. Beyond Wroxham there is virtually no tidal influence, and there are not many fish either except perhaps at the upper limit of navigation, Horstead Mill, Coltishall, where a few good pike (bream too) inhabit the mill pool. One day in early June I spotted a twenty plus in shallows; on June 16th it had gone.

But I digress. Tide tables, as I've said, are invaluable to a Broads angler but they cannot take account of the weather at sea, where a strong north-westerly wind can back it up, causing the tides to flow upriver considerably higher and further than usual. When this condition coincides with a 'spring' tide, floods (sometimes serious ones) occur and fish trapped in dykes and boatbasins sometimes die in thousands, having been taken unawares by the suddenness of the flood. This happens to fish despite their having an instinct (developed over many years) for avoiding trouble, as well as a certain degree of immunity to salt water. All you can do in this situation is head upstream, but of course chocolate-coloured water caused by inland storms does nothing to help your chances. Dykes and boatyards are your best bet – provided permission to fish is given.

Mention of dykes and boatyards prompts me to warn you of a lesser, but still significant, movement of fish that get a taste of salt – just enough perhaps to put them off the feed temporarily but not enough to alarm them. They move out of the river into dykes leading to boatyards and basins, and the slightly salty water passes them by.

They will probably move back into the river to feed as soon as the ebb tide flushes out the salt. The fish also move out of the river into these places for shelter under boat sheds and moored boats during during a persistent east wind which drops the level of the North Sea. Consequently the water gets low and clear up to the tidal limits.

Outbreaks of prymnesium, confined to the Upper Thurne System, causes a mass movement in that area. Some fish get trapped, cannot move and die. Quite a few escape, however. Depending on just where the pollution starts, they either flee down the river Thurne or to a couple of fresh water inlets where the pollution is diluted. No, I don't intend to tell you where these inlets are; those fish are in no condition to withstand being caught. Unfortunately this doesn't stop a few unprincipled characters who, by accident or design, have discovered these places and taken unfair advantage of it.

The movement just described, whilst considerable, is local and a fairly recent phenomenon. However, the next and last one, the autumn migration, has been going on probably for centuries and takes place throughout the whole Broads area; but oddly enough not on *all* the Broads. Fish stay put in shallow broads like Hoveton, Black Horse, Ranworth (excepting a salt tide), Bridge and Cockshoot, all of which, incidentally, are private. On deeper Broads, like Wroxham and Salhouse, they move out, generally in October, and take up winter residence in the more sheltered regions of the river Bure at Wroxham or Horning. Pike of course must go where the food fish go.

As far as the Upper Thurne System is concerned during the October to March period, I feel something similar happens. I have had less experience of fishing the area, but my duties as a bailiff with Anglian Water included relief patrols (my full-time beat was the Middle Bure) and netting and survey work, so I was in the picture. I can tell you that in the winter the top end of Somerton Dyke is thick with bream. Where do you think they have come from? The pike on the adjoining Broads seem to vanish. Where do you think they have gone to? Exactly! The rest is up to you. The cat is out of the bag!

There is also a big concentration of fish in the sheltered reach of the Thurne between the two bridges at Potter Heigham. Twenty-plus pike are caught here every year at this time. The large boat basin here also holds lots of wintering fish. I believe these Potter fish have moved up the Thurne in advance of the high flood tides. The old narrow bridge at Potter helps to hold back much of the detrimental effect of these tides.

Well, that is about it. There's a lot to learn isn't there? Let me try to make it easier for you. I have been asked to give a brief account of my pike fishing experiences on the Broads over a period of about twenty years, during which time I caught about fifty pike, over twenty pounds with a best of 32 lb, plus hundreds of doubles.

During these reflections, I will recall certain facets of the weather, tides, water conditions and fish migrations (regular and otherwise) that I was to learn and turn to my advantage – things seldom mentioned in most of the literature on Broads fishing, yet it is vital information. Without it the odds are 10 to 1 against you. You are most likely to end up fishing for pike where they ain't.

You remember I nearly caught a good pike by accident on Wroxham Broad whilst roach fishing. I thought I had it made: first class pike fishing on the doorstep – who needs the Upper Thurne System? Well, within a month I ended up 'fishing where they ain't'. I think you will find it interesting and informative to read how I eventually caught up with them again, how I learnt to keep in touch and cut down the number of days of sport I would otherwise have lost.

TWENTY YEARS BROADS PIKE FISHING

After losing that biggish Wroxham pike, I concealed my keepnet containing a dozen good livebait in the reeds that evening and returned early next morning armed with pike tackle. 'Might as well have a go until it's time to grab myself a slice of the real action on the old Upper Thurne System' I thought to myself. But sitting in my favourite spot in the reedy bay I didn't exactly slaughter 'em. In fact, by lunch time I'd caught nothing. So I had my lunch and decided to 'do different'.

Changing the position of the no. 6 trebles on the 4 oz baits from top and bottom, to fore and aft. I slid the floats carefully down the 12 lb BS Maxima line, a couple of feet to just clear the silt on the bottom of the shallows. I was to head off on the short row. It was Saturday, change over day at the boat hirers and their customers were either coming or going. For a couple of hours the shallows, averaging three to four feet deep, would be quiet and hopefully productive.

Considering it was my first time and I was unfamiliar with the odd little hidden contours and depressions, on my second slow troll round with baits about 15 and 25 yards astern, the nearest one was taken with confidence. Shipping the oars and webbing up the rod, the drift of the boat tightened the line as the pike turned away and I felt it kick. It had virtually hooked itself with the flank treble in the scissors, the lip treble being free. Using this method, this was to happen almost invariably. Occasionally, but not often, the other line would pose problems if the struck pike was big and lively, but the advantages of having two baits out set to fish differently far outweighed the slight risks involved. Once, however, I hooked two large, lively pike at once. That did give me bother.

This particular pike weighed 14 lb. Shortly afterwards I took another of about 8 lb. Pike obviously under 10 lb were not weighed but slipped straight back, and it wasn't long before I stopped weighing pike less than 20 lb.

But that was it for the day as a battleship thundered through the

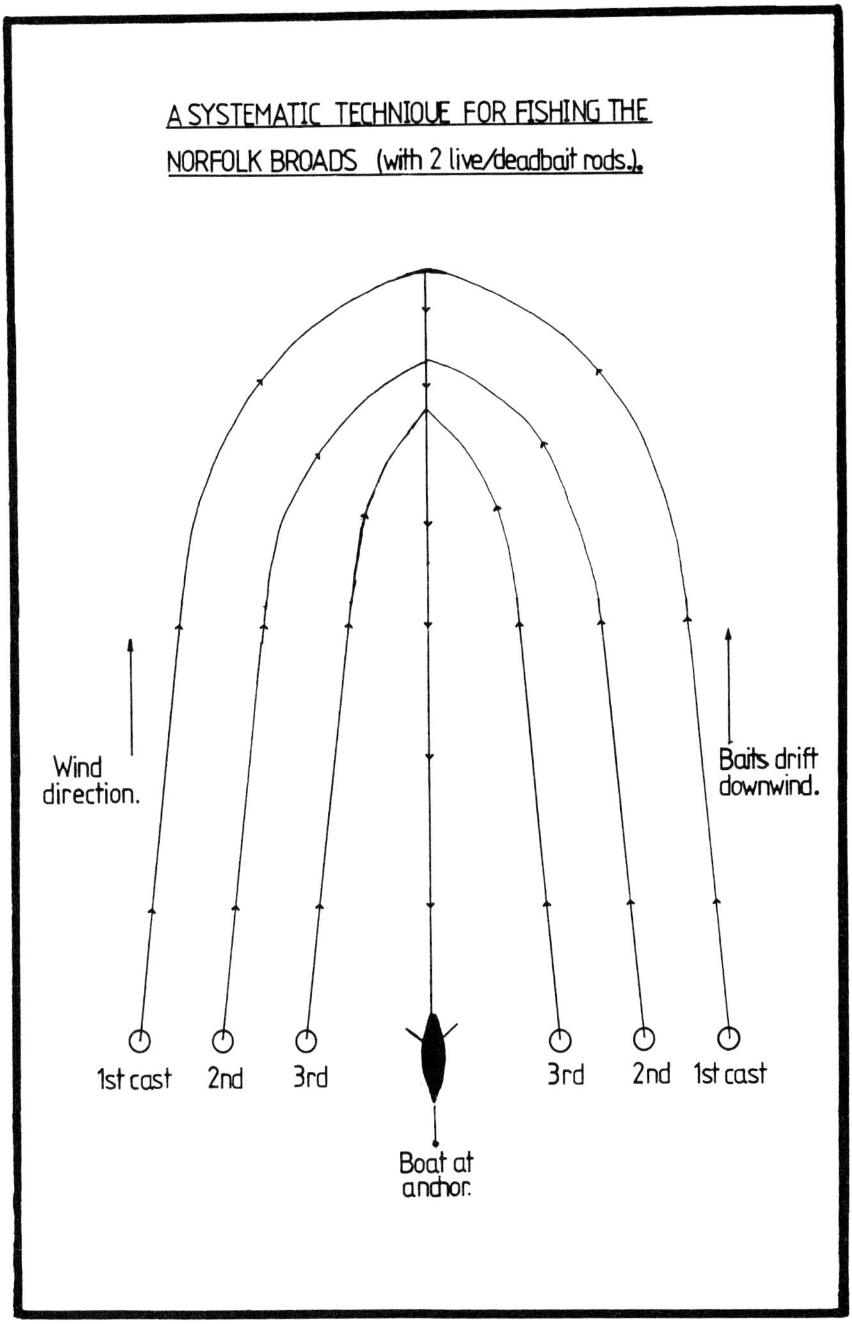

A SYSTEMATIC TECHNIQUE FOR FISHING THE
NORFOLK BROADS (with 2 live/deadbait rods.).
Wind
direction.
Baits drift
downwind.
1st cast
2nd
3rd
3rd
2nd
1st cast
Boat at
anchor.

south entrance of the Broad and bore menacingly for the shallows on an erratic, and what could have been a collision, course. I was seen, however, the steering was over compensated and immediately the Yatch Club HQ came under threat. This danger, too was averted; with the possible consideration that there were to many objects in the way on the Broad a course was set north/north-east for Wroxham town, leaving the low, narrow bridge deeply scarred but still standing.

I left too, thinking perhaps September was a little too early for piking on the open waters of the Broads unless one came down for a few hours or confined one's activities to the isolated little bays. But generally speaking, static pike fishing did not match up to mobile methods.

I tried a variation of this method which proved very successful on fairly windy days when the bottom was reasonably deep and of a uniform level. I would often try it when having lunch or simply taking a rest. I would anchor up with my back to the wind and cast baits, hooked lips and flanks set to just drag bottom, say 10 yards to the left and right, slightly deeper if the wind was very strong. The bow in the line would drag the baits round in front of me whereupon I would cast again a few yards further, continuing this to the limit of my casting ability or until hitting an obvious hotspot.

This method often picks up a pike or two on dour days when they are disinclined to feed, and yet find it impossible to resist having a go at an apparently disabled fish bouncing along the bottom.

In fact, I used this method the following Saturday morning on Wroxham shallows, using small baits because the bottom is composed of mud and silt areas. I had the place to myself until lunch time and made the most of it, as I managed to boat two double and several smaller fish. Then there was a blank spell, followed by the arrival of a couple of day launches which stirred things up a bit, so I moved to my reedy bay, had lunch and replenished my dwindling livebait supply.

I was soon to discover that, as on many other Broads with deeps, shallows and 'in betweens', when the weather was normal far more pike were to be caught in the shallows, providing disturbances were minimal. With a sharp drop in temperature, strong wind or disturbances the pike would move into slightly deeper water, but seldom into the deeps (ten to eleven feet on Wroxham). It was the second week in October and I was becoming increasingly pleased as the number of holiday boats were noticeably decreasing. My catches (both in numbers and in size) were increasing: best pike 21 lb and 22 lb 12 oz. It was also getting colder but I didn't mind in the least – I just wrapped up a bit more.

The following morning there was a fairly sharp frost and, despite trying several different methods, I never got so much as a bite. Obviously, I thought, the frost had put them off. Never mind, 'they'll feed again when it warms up'. They didn't, you know, at least not on Wroxham Broad – because they weren't there any more.

Other anglers plugging up and down in row boats shared the same experience, until by the end of October I was the only one left – except, that is, for two mates who had booked a week's piking holiday on the strength of what they had read. At the end of the week they left without experiencing a single run. Although I continued to fish the area, I fared likewise. Not even a roach either: such a pity – in view of the fact that half a mile away the river was thick with fish. There was nobody to tell *me* what I am now telling you.

I didn't start my bailiff's job until 1962, when I began to learn about fish movements on the broads. In fact, it was quite by chance that I discovered why fish couldn't be caught in Wroxham Broad (and certain other places) when the water temperature dropped to a certain level.

Only a few places are accessible by road on the broads. The half mile or so of the river Bure in Wroxham is one of these places. Consequently it gets a lot of attention from the local roach and bream anglers fishing from the bank.

Summer and winter, these fish are there. In late autumn and winter, however, fishing improves dramatically and excellent catches of bream and roach are made. Yet I never saw a pike caught, despite frequently walking the stretch whilst my wife was shopping.

The bulging keepnets of the roach and bream anglers were obvious. Pike anglers, at least in pre-camera-mania days, were loath to advertise their catches. Then one day, during the last weekend of the season, I met one with whom I was slightly acquainted and managed to get him to talk. This is what he told me:

> We don't bother to fish pike until about the middle of October. There's too many boats and not many pike. Then, when the boats start going, the pike start coming and the word gets around. Don't know why, maybe it's bacause at the same time suddenly there's more roach and bream in the river as well. Well, let's put it this way, you won't hear me grumbling. Come to that, you won't hear me boasting either.

I got the message, and didn't press him further. He had told me plenty. Things were going to be different next season.

Opinions differ locally as to the reason for this mass annual movement of fish where salt water penetration is usually minimal (Broads fish have developed a certain tolerance to small doses). Some believe the clarity of the water on the Broads in late autumn to winter drives the prey fish to the more sheltered, built up river reaches, with their riverside bungalows, boat-sheds, moored craft and so on. Others believe that the lack of natural food in the deeper Broads causes them to move to places where they know they will be fed by anglers and old dears feeding the ducks and swans.

For myself, I don't know. It also happens on the Upper Thurne

System where the salt count is naturally much higher than elsewhere. Here it seems the roach and bream leave Hickling, Heigham and Horsey down Candle Dyke, turning right for Potter Heigham and the sheltered stretch between the two bridges and the adjacent boatyards, or left for Somerton Dyke where they are joined by fish off Martham Broad. Naturally, where the roach and bream go, the pike follow – and the next season I, clued up, followed the pike.

They did the vanishing trick a bit later the following October. It was during the last week, being a bit milder than the previous time. Five visits paid to the Broad produced thirty-six pike, twenty-eight of them doubles with two over 20 lb. This high average weight was to be a pleasing feature throughout my Broad piking campaign. This time I didn't hang about, one blank session was enough to send me chasing after them to Wroxham.

Sport was so good that it was a routine I was to follow for several years. Each season would produce several pike over 20 lb and lots of upper doubles, and I knew it was only a matter of time before that thirty would show up. One day I hooked it, but it threw the hooks at the net. Any thoughts I may once have cherished of fishing the Upper Thurne System faded away.

During this period the most memorable day's sport I had was when nearly all the action took place in one hour, when I was supposed to be resting and having lunch after spending the morning trolling two livebaits up and down the river in my normal fashion. I anchored up just off a dyke entrance, put on a couple of fresh livebaits hooked pectoral and dorsel and lobbed them out a few yards to the dyke mouth.

The first bait was taken whilst the second was still in mid air, and that's how it went until eleven pike had been boated. On one occasion two pike were on at the same time. All but one were doubles to 18 lb 8 oz and one pike was caught twice. Then the sport ended as abruptly as it began. Perhaps I had caught them all.

I did find that such places were often hotspots, particularly towards the end of the season, and at times pike were to be found well up these dykes adjacent to such things as moored craft and boatsheds. But I always asked permission when in doubt, or when fishing from a private bank, and it was never refused.

Bridge Broad, just above Wroxham Bridge, produces pike over 20 lb every season and is particularly good because of the moored craft when the river runs very clear with low temperatures and/or east winds. But I understand that nowadays, because of a few irresponsible anglers, permission to fish is only given to boat hirers.

I would have been quite happy to have carried on fishing the Wroxham area indefinitely, but inevitably my methods and catches were noted and gradually more and more pikers hired boats and joined in. There was still plenty of room, especially since we bailiffs started

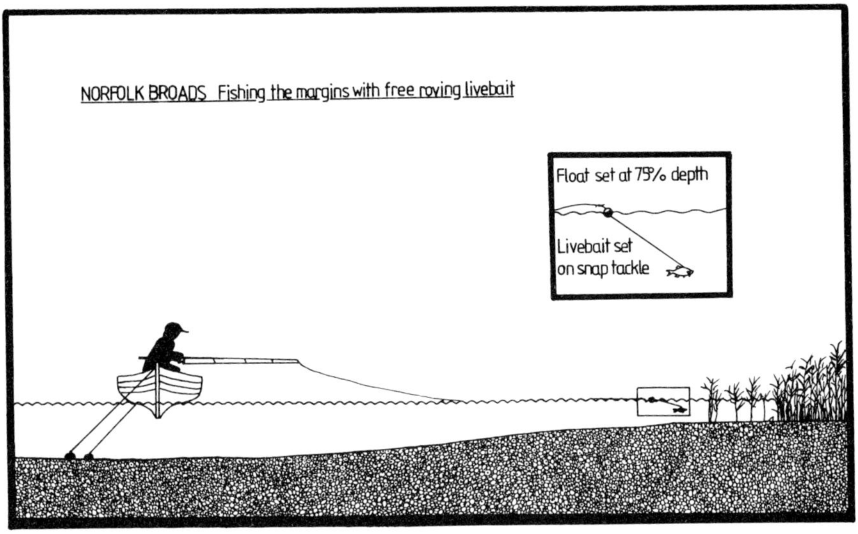

working weekends and taking time off during the week, but I was a bit spoilt and a couple of other anglers on the water at the same time as me constituted a crowd. So, eventually, I decided a change of venue was due.

There are a few pike here and above Wroxham. The sheltered reach at Belaugh holds a few, as does the S-bend a couple of hundred yards below the old boatyard at Coltishall, whilst Horstead mill-pond harbours a few – and a few very big bream. But I don't rate the area very highly and would not recommend it to the holiday angler whose time is limited.

The five river miles from Wroxham downstream to Horning offered promise. However, about halfway lay Salhouse Broad on the right of the river and, opposite on the left, Hoveton Great broad which, however, is inaccessible from the river Bure and strictly private. I thought I would give Salhouse Broad a look first, and try to get permission to fish Hoveton Great Broad at the same time.

A local chap who collected mooring/fishing fees from the holiday makers on Salhouse Broad told me that the pike fishing wasn't what it used to be. In fact, I found it disappointing with regard to the pike, although on very small roach livebaits I caught several perch in excess of 2 lb. But it wasn't perch I was after and when Mr Blofeld's keeper finally gave me the all clear I gave a donation to his favourite charity, borrowed one of his punts and got cracking on Hoveton Great Broad – and had a great time whilst it lasted.

It is a fairly large, beautiful Broad with a secluded secretive atmosphere and fairly reeks of pike – big pike. 'This is where I get my thirty,' I told myself. The late Dennis Pye used to catch some of his great Hickling pike here and so did a few others. It is very shallow for the most part, only going down to four feet at the deepest end where it meets the shut-off dyke which connects it to the river. Dennis once told me that one winter in the shallowest of corners big bream were shoaled up so thick you could walk on them.

This is one of the Broads that hold their fish throughout the year – possibly because it is sufficiently shallow with much rich silt, to retain enough natural food to keep the fish going throughout the winter. It was my intention to investigate further but unfortunately my stay there was rather brief.

I paid the place several visits and caught some cracking pike with a higher average weight even than Wroxham, with two at 25 lb plus. It was too shallow really to practise my favourite trolling method, but I did well drifting the baits around in the wind at the deep end. Usually I was the only person on the Broad and enjoyed it immensely. There was always that feeling of excitement and anticipation seldom equalled elsewhere.

Imagine my disappointment when on two consecutive weekdays the gamekeeper told me that I couldn't come because a 'special party' was arriving to fish. It may have been rather churlish of me but I thought 'That's it', and never went again. As it happens, it was also rather hasty of me. The day after I fished it for the last time, somebody caught a thirty-seven at the dam end. I wished I hadn't sent that letter to the keeper.

About half a mile further down the river on the right is Decoy Broad with the fishing rights held by the Norwich and District Angling Association. It is cut off from the river and fishing is only by boats owned by the above. Outsiders can fish it provided they join the Association and pay for the hire of a boat. Fees are very reasonable, but avoid weekends when boats may all be booked for matches. Fish are present throughout the year. They can't get out or in since the Nature Trust dammed the entrance in the interests of rare water plants.

I mustn't tell you any more about Decoy, beyond that I fished it happily and successfully for several more years after catching that thirty without ever catching another, but I got very close once or twice. As far as I know, the monster was never seen again.

What reason did I have this time for leaving yet another productive pike venue? It stopped producing, that's why! When the entrance was blocked, at the time of year when fish would be expected to enter, I experienced three consecutive blank sessions. Other anglers shared the experience. That was enough for me. But again, I may have been too hasty. I heard recently that pike are again being caught there, including a thirty.

The next move was downriver a mile or so to the Horning-Woodbastwick reaches, bypassing Blackhorse or Hoveton Little Broad – a very good pike water but strictly private and also owned by the late Mr

Blofeld with whose keeper I'd blotted my copybook. It is open to holiday boaters, who often ignore the signs and poach it, as do people who should know better, and they get into trouble when they are caught. Big pike caught here, as at Hoveton Great Broad, are usually described as being caught on Wroxham Broad at times when there are no fish on the Broad.

This latest move was to further my education in the problem of mass fish movements on the Broads – this time caused by salt penetration. I have already written at length about it and intend to write little more. But, you ask – how can you tell there is salt in the water? Good question. I asked Jed and he told me that if he suspected the salt was up he would walk up or down the river tasting it until he had pinpointed the extent and the strength of it. I looked at him closely, but his leathery old face remained inscrutable.

Actually if you dip your finger in and put it to your lips it *can* be tasted. But bear in mind that the flood tide flows faster toward the bottom. It follows, therefore, that that is where the salt is strongest.

Personally, I prefer to follow the roach and bream anglers upriver. The areas where they are catching will mark the limits of salt penetration. There should be a lot of fish there, pushed up from the lower reaches – and that includes pike. Excellent catches are often made in these times, but usually it doesn't last long. With tides returning to normal fish drop back to where they came from. But, as I wrote earlier, only so far.

The Horning-Woodbastwick stretch fished much like Wroxham with regard to quantity and quality except for one important consideration: salt, of course. By October, the resident shoals are normally reinforced by masses of fish from the lower regions of the Bure, fish which are conditioned to move up in advance of the forthcoming high and salty tides. (Some go straight up the river Thurne to Potter Heigham and further.)

You can almost guarantee that during the pike season there will be an occasion when a salt surge is powerful enough to send the fish fleeing to Wroxham. They don't seem to like staying in the open river and, once pushed beyond Horning, don't stop until they reach Wroxham, where anglers reap the benefits.

With falling tides they usually drop back after a few days, sometimes after a few weeks, occasionally longer. Once, in fact, they disappeared just after Christmas and never came back for the rest of the season – which, incidentally, convinced me that another move was due. And this time it was a long one.

Under normal conditions, however, all that happens with these somewhat fluctuating tides is a to and fro-ing of the fish stocks between Horning Ferry and Horning Swan, a distance of about half a mile. Dry keepnets at the former means wet ones at the latter, at the upriver end, so you just keep your eyes and ears open. Horning Swan Bend is usually the limit of tidal and salt influences, though now and again fish are pushed round the Bend and up the river to the end of Horning, Black Horse Broad Dyke.

When this happens, some of the fish enter Ropes Hill Dyke and the dykes on Crabbetts Marsh. I have had good sport in these places occasionally when the river has been very slow. The banks are all private, however, and the owners, who usually live away, are perfectly entitled to ask you to untie your ropes from their bank.

The Horning-Woodbastwick reaches provide excellent sport, particularly during October when masses of fish are coming through from lower down. I would often dispense with my boat and sit in ambush on the Woodbastwick bank, opposite Horning Ferry, and have the time of my life. On one occasion landing a twenty-four, a twenty-three and a half, and half a dozen good doubles in a morning before they passed on.

There is about half a mile of bank fishing available for those without a boat and it is well worth a visit at the right time. But beware, the access road from Woodbastwick village is subject to flooding. If the road has a couple of inches of water at the bottom of the ebb it will probably have a foot or more at the top of the tide and may not run off for some time. You could be stranded. In any case, such a situation could mean no fish, as I have explained. So get back in your car and motor off to Wroxham where limited bank fishing is available.

There is another little snag. Avoid boat fishing the area at weekends. What little traffic there is in winter is concentrated there due to the comings and goings from the many boatyards in the area, and the Yacht Club hold races there on Sundays. I will mention a better place to spend a weekend pike fishing later on.

Several more years concentrating on the Horning and Wroxham pike added considerably to my tally of twenties and my general knowledge and I was happy with the situation. Then one day I realised I shouldn't have been. 'What's happened to my ambition? 'I asked myself. I had got my thirty and knew I was in with a chance of a forty. So is everyone who fishes the right way, at the right time in the right place, between Horning and Wroxham. The trouble was, I wasn't working hard enough at it. I was getting old and lazy. I excused myself by reasoning that even if I did work hard a forty was just as likely to fall to a keen young first-timer with sound tackle who had read the right material. And it would serve me right.

Then I experienced that almost totally blank end-of-season session at Woodbastwick and my mind was made up. It was time for off. Anglian Water, convinced that only a long rest could cure my nervous rash, kindly pensioned me off a little prematurely, so I was free to take up a new challenge. LAA talent scouts got wind of this, decided it was an opportunity not to be missed and offered me incentives I couldn't refuse – money. Lo and behold, I was a bailiff again on Lenwade lakes. There

I saw a carp that was to take years off my life – five to be precise, but that's another story.

Anyway, I haven't quite finished with the other one yet. During the time I was fishing the H Wick area, in slack periods such as when salt tides mucked things up a bit, I did a bit d/s as far as South Walsham Broad and up the Ant to Wayford Bridge and beyond. I didn't rate it very highly. For someone with only a week to spend I'd suggest he would be better off visiting Horning and Wroxham.

Downstream from Horning Ferry lies Cockshoot Broad, a nature reserve, and unfortunately STRICTLY PRIVATE. A bit further down Ramworth Dyke leads to Ramworth and Malthouse Broad, the former leased by N and DAA system, as Decoy Broad, and a shadow of its former self. Malthouse Broad gives poor fishing and is hopeless after salt tides begin. Nearer the sea the situation deteriorates. South Walsham Dyke and Broad is a waste of time from October onwards, and not much better before then.

Going up the river Ant, keep going until you come to Barton Broad and don't stop if it is later than October. Follow the fish up Lime Kibre Dyke to Neatishead, where you will be pelted with abuse and maggots by hostile natives in the restricted space available.

Turn your boat round, 'Oops, careful', and do the same at the top left-hand corner of the Broad, where you will have to pay a small sum to a Mr Cox at his boatyard.

It would have been better if had you carried straight on through Barton and turned right up Stalham Dyke, quickly passing (if you are wise) Sutton Dyke on the right, before finding yourself confronted by legions of tired, battered craft moored up in Stalham boatyard. Here and there you will see a fishing rod sticking out, whilst mechanics, cleaning women and odd bods scurry about. Dally a while and drink in the scenery before turning round and going back the way you came – until you reach the Ant again. Turn right and proceed to Wayford Bridge (which miraculously still stands) and moor up at the pub moorings. Go and have a good nosh up and then get sloshed.

If you wake up in the morning determined to go fishing despite the hangover, change your cruiser for a rowboat and row it quietly up towards Horning Rock or the Dilham Canal. Shallow and narrow, most large craft avoid it and you might just get lucky slowly trolling a small bait upstream or drifting it back downstream. On the other hand, you may get unlucky. Remember, I said *most* large craft avoid it.

If you've gathered that I don't rate the Ant waterways very highly, you're absolutely right.

If for any reason you should need a change (even throughout the winter the volume of boat traffic at popular centres like Horning and Wroxham can be sufficient reason) I can recommend the Filly, Ormsley and Rollesly group of Broads just a few miles away, with just a small dyke called Muckfleet connecting them to the river Bure below Acle. The only boats are rowboats which are hired to anglers, a couple of rescue launches and some yachts which are no problem in the large area of water. The scenery is very pleasant and the atmosphere tranquil, the sort of setting pictured and described in the Broads holiday brochures. The fishing is good too and responds well to the methods I have described, though few seem to practise it there. A twenty is always on the cards, a thirty quite possible (there are more caught than reported) and I am convinced that in those hundreds of acres of water at least one record pike prowls.

In drawing to a close may I say that I have tried to strike the right balance between what you must know, should know and could know, plus a little light relief.

I am sure what I have written will increase your chances considerably if you put it into practice when you fish the Broads. But for heaven's sake come properly prepared. A number of pike caught by myself and friends had been hooked and lost by other anglers using line or traces or hooks far too frail for the job. Remember, the smaller the hook the thinner the wire. I now use 15 b/s line, 20 b/s traces and nothing smaller than size 6 trebles and don't think it's a bit too heavy. Why spend years after your first twenty or thirty and then lose it unnecessarily because of a weak spot in your tackle. A big pike will always find it, believe me.

Always tighten up your line until you 'feel' the pike before striking or rather 'pulling' the hooks home.

Play a pike by 'backwinding' if your check is the least bit unreliable and try to avoid giving slack line. Most snap tackles bought have the wire passed only once or twice round the hook shank, on the strike the top treble slips down the wire and fails to bite home. I have seen this happen many times. The wire must be passed round at least four times.

After assembling your tackle attach it by the hooks to something substantial and really test it. Far better something breaks now than when attached to your 'fish of a life time'.

If you believe that pike, like anglers, like to assemble under the shadow of a riverside pub – good luck to you. But if catching them is your top priority, then you will have to put yourself about a bit.

And don't leave it too long. Dora, the last of the great Broads leviathans, the most celebrated and fished for, photographed and fought over of them all, and currently being pursued from Marthan to Hickling via Heigham and Horsey and back again by a handful of the top boys and a bunch of no hopers will finally run out of steam and roll over. The fun will have ended.

The earlier drop outs from the Upper Thurne System, already practising their undoubted talents in the Middle Bure System, will be reinforced by even more determined and ambitious lads whose philosophy is 'who dares wins' – and you'd better believe it.

For the moment there is room enough and pike enough for everybody, but I fear that increasing angling pressures on the Middle Bure System will ultimately lead to another Upper Thurne System situation. With less pike to be caught, the competition will be fierce.

Get up there as soon as you can – and good fishing!

Exploring Irish Waters

BILL WINSHIP

GENERAL INTRODUCTION

With over 600,000 acres of still water and 9,000 miles of rivers, Ireland offers the angler more possibilities than anyone could ever hope to explore in a single lifetime. The geographic scale of these waters means that in practical terms one can only ever hope to fish a tiny fraction of what is available.

Furthermore, the task of describing the Irish pike scene is greatly complicated by the wide assortment of waters available, ranging from the sluggish reed-fringed streams of the central plain to the rocky gale-blasted mountain loughs of Co. Mayo. Most of these waters contain pike, but not all of them produce big pike worthy of special attention. The aim of the chapter is to identify some of the better waters and to put forward our approach to exploring an approach which has resulted in us catching some big pike up to 20 lb.

The famous pike historian, Fred Buller, had left us in no doubt that historically the largest pike have been produced from the great limestone loughs of Corrib, Mask and Conn. Most of these 'mammoth' pike were caught before the Inland Fisheries Trust began their pike netting operations and few pike anglers now bother with the western loughs, even though they still contain big pike.

Modern pike anglers now tend to concentrate on the massive Shannon system, fishing waters like Lough Allen, Ree, Derg, Key and Gara, all of which support plenty of big predators. In the north, lower and upper Lough Erne are noted waters, as are the tributaries of the great Lough Neagh which has recently produced large numbers of specimen pike. To the south and east the river Barrow and its feeder streams can provide good sport, but this area is dominated by trout interests. Few pike are returned to the water alive yet those which do survive sometimes attain goodly proportions – in fact, the river Barrow has produced some of the largest river pike ever taken in Ireland, including the river record of 42 lb.

With so many legendary pike waters available the visiting angler is confronted with an attractive range of alternatives, any one of which promises a genuine chance of good sport.

MAP SHOWING SOME OF THE MAIN PIKE LOUGHS AND RIVERS IN IRELAND

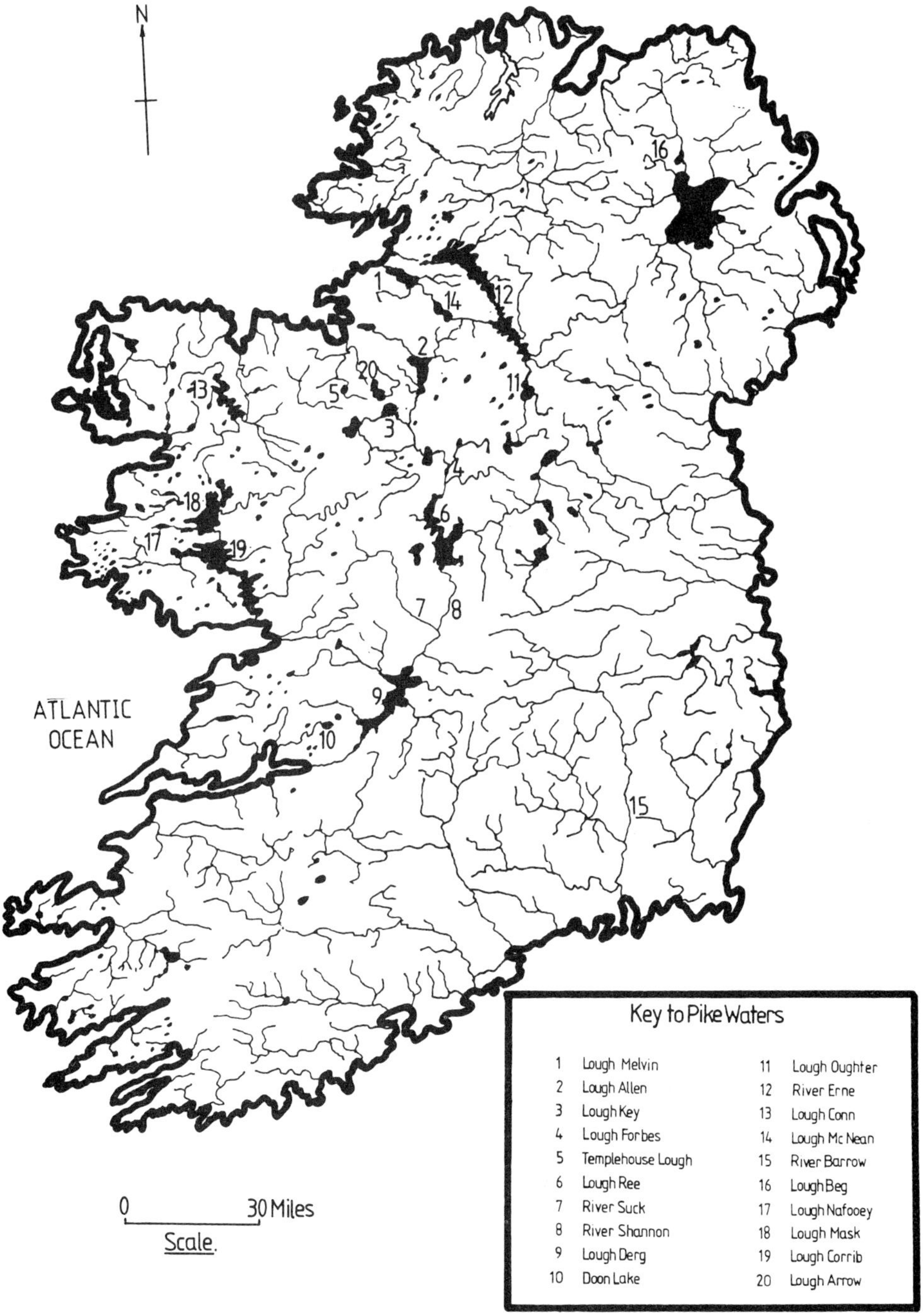

PLANNING A TRIP

To help sort out the best waters the Irish Tourist Board have produced an excellent freshwater coarse angling guide book which provides useful details about many of the best waters. This information has been reconstructed on the map (p. 59) but even these well proven waters should be checked in advance because sporting prospects can change from year to year and a little research can help to make sure you fish in the right place at the right time.

Checking can be done by contacting local Irish boatmen and anglers well before actually setting dates or venues. This kind of detailed forward planning is useful because even Irish waters are not so easy to fish, and are seldom so plentifully stocked that they give themselves up without effort on your part. In any case, after investing your savings on a week's fishing it is important to get things right.

Fortunately the Irish people make great hosts. Their sociability and warmth is legendary and they are often surprisingly helpful in providing angling information. They will often make angling needs their own business, as part of good service. It is rare to find a hotelier or guest house proprietor who knows about the pike angler's needs, yet they will invariably know someone who does and will make it their business to find out what you need to know. Irish people are very generous in sharing angling information; quite different to the more secretive English pike scene.

Although it is difficult to overstate the importance of forward planning there are times when even the best planned trips go awry. Unforeseen conditions can result in a whole week of blank sessions. Such disasters should be viewed with an air of detachment as they are inevitable; they happen to everyone sooner or later. The following account recalls a fishing trip to Lough Allen when everything went according to plan.

LOUGH ALLEN

Lough Allen lies at the head of the famous Shannon system in Co. Leitrim. It is fed by four rivers and, over seven miles long, is one of the larger Irish loughs. It contains trout, rudd, bream, eels, rudd-bream hybrids, perch and some very large pike approaching record proportions.

This lough is one of the best pike waters in Europe and enjoys an illustrious history of big catches. It was no lesser an angler than Clive Gammon who caught three 20 lb pike on successive days, whilst one London angler actually caught four 20 lb fish in a single session. These reports, along with many others, have attracted pike anglers to Lough Allen on what have become for many something of an annual pilgrimage.

IRISH LOUGHS   Why large waters tend to produce the most big pike

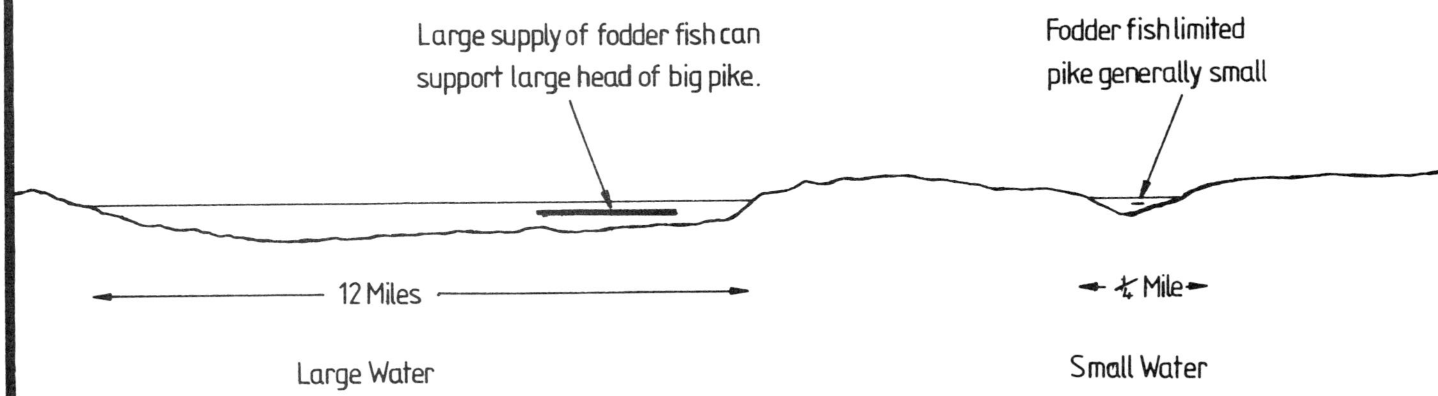

Hardly specimen class but fish like this can give a foretaste of things to come. These pike were caught on Lough Mask which is one of the most exciting but dangerous waters to fish. This part of the lough is full of pike and deadly rocks. (Photo: B. Winship)

Eight weeks prior to our first visit we contacted some people in the Drumshanbo area to secure accommodation. In our letter of enquiry we made clear our intention to fish for pike and asked for details of the location and whereabouts of the Lough Allen pike. Soon afterwards our host confirmed our provisional booking but regretted that he had no real knowledge about the seasonal movements of Lough Allen pike; he would try to find out. Of course we thought we had heard the last on the subject, but three weeks later a brown envelope postmarked Eire dropped through the letter-box with an audible thud. The envelope contained photos and details of big Allen pike caught in recent years. Best of all though, a hand drawn sketch map was enclosed, detailing many of the Lough Allen pike holding areas. Armed with this information we found ourselves in a state of premature readiness; we couldn't wait to get amongst those big Allen pike.

Our first morning on Lough Allen was like a dream come true. It was still springtime yet the humid warmth of the atmosphere was more reminiscent of June than April. All our instincts told us we were in for a good day's sport as similar conditions in the past had been very productive.

With high-running expectations we rowed our boat quietly out of Bellantra Bay trolling two spoon baits in the wake of the boat. The rods

Bill Winship holds a big pike taken on Lough Allen. Fish like this one make all the preparation worthwhile. (Photo: B. Winship)

were nodding attentively to the flickering rolling action of our spoon baits. We regulated our boat speed by the working action of the baits: too fast and the rod tip just pulled over, too slow and the spoons started to grab the lough bed. Fortunately we used the weedless spoons so we never lost any lures at all.

By 11 o'clock four pike up to a weight of 11 lb had responded to our wobbling, flashing ABU Giller lures. They were all lean rapacious fish, typical of the Lough Allen fish we had already seen in various photographs. Feeling pleased we returned to Bellantra bridge where we had lunch and met an elderly German who was eel fishing. Over tea and sandwiches he advised us that the bay adjacent to the Arigna river was the best place for pike.

A two mile row to this bay found us tired and boat weary so we quietly beached the boat and decided to fish with deadbaits for a rest and a change. At least, that is what was intended. In the event we walked to a point of the river some hundred yards from the river mouth and cast out the trout deadbaits. Within seconds the float cocked just beneath the water and began to twitch its way along the river margin, towed along by an unseen force. A firm strike was countered by violent head shakes as a big fish surged off out of the river towards the open lough. After a dogged twenty minute struggle, a lean 44 inch-long pike was netted, weighing in at 21 lb.

After releasing this fish we tried the same routine and another pike came from exactly the same point in the river. The second fish was smaller, weighing in at 14 lb. We never did get another chance to rest that day. We returned to our hotel exhausted yet, above all, thoroughly delighted with our good fortune.

Later in the week we fished the northern end of the lough and caught some perch on spinners and an 18 lb pike in the mouth of the river Shannon. We also found some very large dead pike on the rocky margins. Presumably they had died during spawning earlier in the year. Some of the 'pikey' looking bays that we visited looked ideal for our purposes and in general we found the pike were fairly well distributed across the loch. However, it is worth repeating that up-to-date information of fish movements should be sought to make the most of Lough Allen.

The Western Loughs of Ireland: The Big Conn

BARRIE RICKARDS

I make no apology for the pun of this title, for I begin this essay where I mean to end it, namely on the awful contrast between the captivating beauty of the great western loughs and the mythical beast that forever seems to embrace them. In 1984 I published in the magazine *Course Fisherman* an analysis of pike removal from the Irish waters, gleaned from numerous reports of the then Inland Fisheries Trust. Over a period of about a quarter of a century about *One Million* pike were officially removed, killed and counted. Over the same period the actual tonnage for culling on each water actually increased slightly, and the average size of the pike removed gradually fell, to a consistent figure of about 1½ lb. Of course, inculcated with the idea that all pike were evil, a great many other pike died, unofficially. The only good pike was a dead one; the only good fish a trout. Yet the figures show that all the work was not only totally in vain, but actually made matters worse in that it produced more pike, all capable of eating trout!

The polarisation of standpoints could not be more marked. Here is a country – Mayo, Galway, Clare, Sligo and Roscommon, the very names are magical – which entices pike anglers with its mythical monster, its real monsters, its history, its staggering beauty and its tourist agencies; and it attempts to annihilate that which it uses as bait! It is indeed a con. But times change, the slaughter annually decreases, and a greater realisation of the true role of the pike in these great fisheries is under way. Some of the trout waters where pike killing has stopped are, it seems, better trout waters! There is, however, an interesting quirk to this story. It is this. There can be no doubt that in Ireland all pike have been killed, always. It became a tradition. I have seen this at first hand in the western water, such as Mask, Nafooey, Corrib and Derg. There is no blood lust involved (as happens on trout waters in the UK). It is simply the done thing, done unquestioningly. Yet, those waters have produced some very large pike indeed, certainly in excess of 50 lb weight. I do not myself believe that fish over 60 lb have ever been caught, despite claims of 90 lb fish in the dim and distant past. No fish

Lure fishing from a boat. (Photo: B. Rickards)

of 80 lb has been listed. In other words, the colloquial 'almost a hundred pounds' has been transcribed as 90 lb. Modern work is beginning to suggest that where repeated killing of pike takes place the small number of fish which escape year by year (and perhaps learn to do so) do have a chance of growing very large, perhaps by feeding upon the increased number of jack pike produced by the slaughter.

It is therefore possible that Ireland, and the western loughs in particular, has produced its occasional monster pike of 50 lb, not in spite of the killing, but *because* of it. This makes more sense than ascribing the giants to some unknown water quality or food quality factor. For example, the geological foundation of several of the loughs are quite different; Ree is vastly different from Mask and Corrib for example, and they from Nafooey and Conn. They are all, in a sense, rich waters, but rich as much because of their bigness as of the pH value. There will always be enough food to go round for some – the big ones. Thus whilst pike killing might do little for the quality of trout fishing, and little for the general standards of pike fishing, it might produce a monster – once in a while.

I should nail my own flag to the mast. I do not fish the magical western loughs for fifty pounders, not in this lifetime. I fish them because they are amongst the most spectacular places on earth; and we do not know what pike lie beneath the wind-swept waters. At times on Nafooey, quiet times, the surround of hills gives you that 'feeling very small' feeling which you get when standing alone in a great cavern, or cathedral. On other occasions the wind controls all, waves mix with the dark air, and sodden, lead skies blacken the spirits. Afloat you can be easily frightened. On land you may cringe as you pretend to fish on. Yet an hour later there can be a peace and calm that enables you to appreciate not only the grandeur, but why you are there at all. The pike is an integral element of this wild formula, not merely an incidental. You couldn't get the same understanding playing golf, even whilst sailing – and certainly not whilst fishing for bream. In these places the pike seems the only real quarry appropriate to the majesty.

It is easy to see then why the mythology which is Irish piking finds ready acceptance in the souls of men from towns, and especially if those towns are in the UK. It is equally easy to understand that such places as Derg and Corrib pose a challenge or two to any meek newcomers from the east! In the first place a change in attitude of mind is needed; in the second a rethink on tackle and techniques. It is not easy to fish these big waters from the bank – not unless you have a boat! So you can boat fish or use the boat as access to the most likely bank swims. The boats need to be big, over fifteen feet, and you need a good outboard, oars (preferably attached to thole pins, not rowlocks) and lifejacket. Fortunately lifejackets today will go comfortably under a Barbour jacket and they are increasingly made available even at the

Setting out for a day amongst the Irish pike. (Photo: B. Rickards)

Boathouse in Ireland. (Photo: B. Rickards)

more remote venues. I would never be without one again if afloat on a real water.

In the days of clinker-built boats it was obligatory to have a sponge bottom in the boat – presumably a boat which which didn't need baling out wasn't a real boat. I recall some hair-raising days Charles Morley and I had, trolling the western bays of Lough Ree, when we could see the water seeping between the planks at our feet! Today, of course, fibre rules, and whilst we remain drier I do feel that our equipment – the weight of it – helps stabilise an otherwise skittish creature. There are no real anglers' boats available on these loughs – just good and bad boats which transport anglers – but you do need one . . .

If you need to make a mental adjustment to go afloat then try a few other mental exercises. Get good anchors and 100 feet of rope you can pull (i.e. thick and soft, not hard nylon). Get some thick gloves for doing the job. Get some boat rod rests, and a landing net with a short handle that you can hang on the thole pins. Think boats, think safety. Last of all think pike, and comfort, in that order. I would not be without an echo sounder if I could avoid it; and I possess admiralty charts of all the Irish waters of any size that I have fished.

Remember, when the echo sounder tells you that there are big rocks under the boat, it is too late. I remember once trolling Lough Ree in what I thought was 70 feet of water (misreading the chart), looking over the side and seeing boulders with a diameter of ten feet, their tops only two feet below the surface! I had a similar experience on Corrib, this time misreading the echo sounder. When you fish on your own there is often a lot to pay attention to when afloat.

First of all then, get used to boat fishing, handling the boat, anchoring it, trolling, baitfishing, and spinning from it. One can try a little boat fishing in UK waters, to get used to it, using large gravel pits and rivers; it is that important.

Only then do you begin to think about the actual fishing tackle you need. It is easy to take too much stuff on board – I usually do – but all that is needed is a couple of powerful rods say 2 1/3 lb testcurve) for trolling or boat fishing, and perhaps a third rod to cast and spin with. For the big Irish waters I always upgrade my line strength to 15 lb bs, occasionally to 18 lb bs, partly because I do drop the rod on the gunwhales sometimes, and the same line can get dented without being noticed – it just gives a bit of safety margin. The fighting ability of pike in loughs is no worry to me – they show the full gamut of fantastic to sluggish, simply depending upon when I fish. The nicest time to fish the western loughs is in spring and autumn, when most people fish them of course. At these times the ability of pike to bend your mind, as well as your rod, is legendary; but the same waters respond in winter too, and at those times you may get a more sluggish response. So apart

Fred Wagstaffe and Bob Reynolds on Lough Nafooey. (Photo: B. Rickards)

from strong rods and lines the rest of the tackle can be much the same as you would use in the UK.

In this chapter I need not worry about telling you where to fish (i.e. which water) because all the water I have mentioned, and almost every other lough large and small in western Eire, have good piking and big pike. Where on a particular water should one try? Somebody recently pointed out something to me, of which I was aware, but not in the terms he stated. He said, 'On a new, big water, I would always begin on the bank which the south-west winds blow.' In other words, on the north-east bank, or some bay or other feature at that end, or corner, of the water. When I examined my own approaches to big waters it was exactly the same, though I hadn't thought of it in those terms!

On Lough Derg there are some very good areas in that part of the lough, and also some superb bays all along the eastern shore. Although these may at times take the full push of the winds they do have sheltered corners and reed-lined shores quite superb for trolling. Some of Derg's bays have soft emergent weeds in twelve feet of water. If you find this situation, especially with a river or stream entering, then you have found pike. Other waters seem very barren – Nafooey, for example; but in this case you have no problem, the wind battered eastern end is the place to be, at least in my experience. Mask and Corrib respond similarly – again in my experience – though both these waters have western arms with good reputations.

Two other factors are worth noting on all waters. One is that each water is unique and will have its own hotspots. The second is that pike move house at intervals, most notably in February and March. On Nafooey they may move to the western end of the lough. Pike do not need reed or rush beds to spawn on, and they may choose relatively shallow water packed with soft weeds, or water of twelve feet or so with string weed growth. All depends upon the facilities available to them so suss out those facilities. It used to be that the Cong canal, between Mask and Corrib, was a good bet when it was full of water, the pike (and big trout) moving into shallow water. This would need checking out for it is an area I have not been to for several years now.

Lough Carra is an interesting water in that it is one of the few where the pike tonnage removed in the 1970s actually declined. Whether they opted for a nominal half ton or so I know not, for one can never judge whether the removal effort put in is the same from year to year. However, it does have big pike in it, and it does have an interesting north-east corner with a 'sheltered' western bank. It is similar in shape and disposition to Ardingly Reservoir, though somewhat larger! Some of the best areas are in the same positions, suggesting that wind and water circulation do play a real part.

I think it is obvious from what I have been saying that finding the water and finding the general pikey areas on the water chosen are not really major problems. The real challenge is in becoming good enough, and persistent enough, at boat fishing to be able to troll from the boat, or beach it in the right place for bank fishing; in other words to be effective and efficient. I am assuming at this stage that you have overcome any mental hang ups about big, windy waters and big windy anglers!

Trolling with spoons, spinners and plugs is one of the main methods to use. But by all means troll a dead fish like a trout or mackerel or perch; or attach a perch behind a spoon. You can troll in traditional style, keeping the outboard on a slow tick-over speed, or you can sink and draw the bait by changing the pace. With trolled fish baits you can stop altogether, allowing them to sink. Choice of spoons is difficult – so opt for old favourites: an egg-shaped copper and silver or an elongated silver spoon like a piker or its equivalent. Copper is a good colour on the Irish loughs. Possibly, in the very clear water, it is a little bit more 'natural' in its flash than a silver spoon. Big plugs also work well, but I often think we overdo the size; a lot of big pike in Eire have fallen to small plugs and spinners intended for salmon and trout.

Never ignore the technique of casting from an anchored boat. Quite

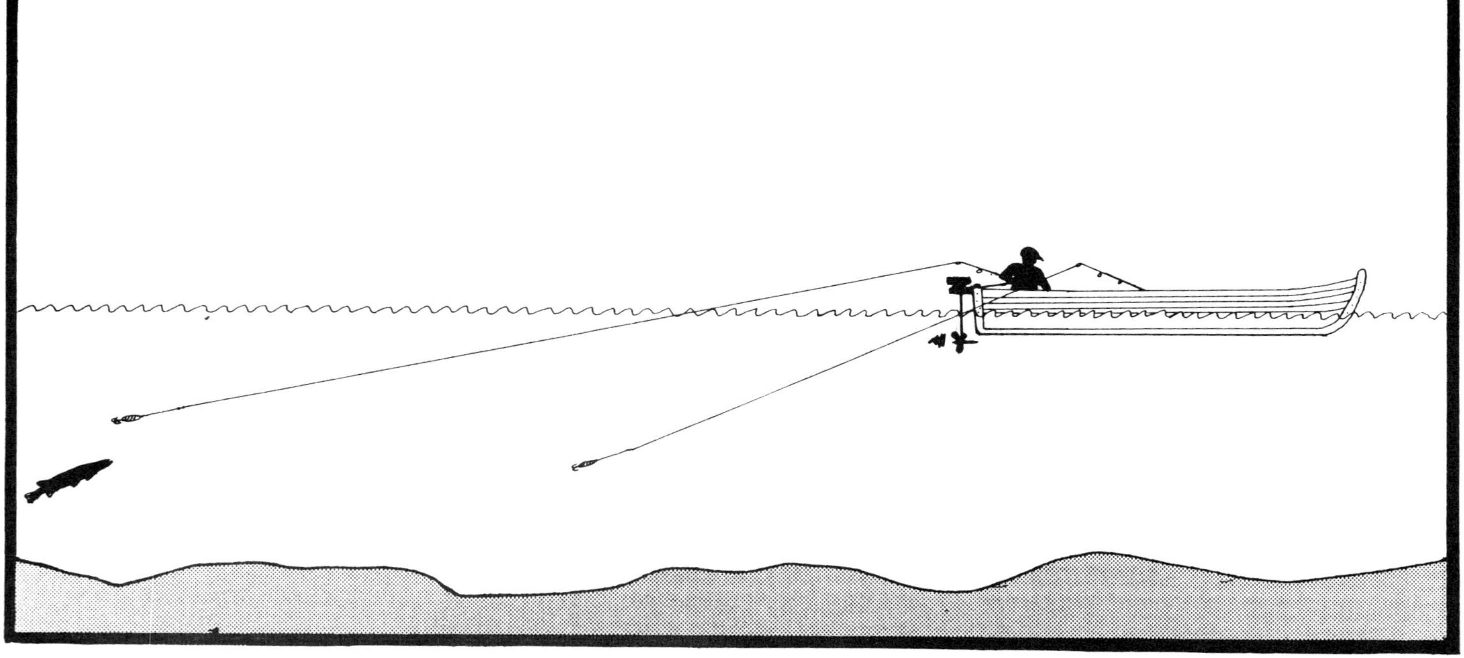

TROLLING: The traditional method for pike fishing on the Irish Loughs.

often you can locate a good area by trolling, yet pick up fish more easily by putting baits on them or throwing a spoon spinner or plug over them. If you are taking them on the troll on deep water then this switch is less easy and best avoided. Trolling techniques need skill and experience and it is beyond our scope here. But note that downrigger systems, whether commercial or DIY are very efficient and get over that awful business of knowing how much line to let out, how much lead to put on, and so forth. Generally the beginner will fish too far behind the boat. I think anything from 5 yards to 25 yards is about correct, depending upon the particular contours; if close and deep, use enough lead up trace to hold it down. You soon get a rationale of your own worked out, but with two of you the team work needs to be planned carefully in advance. Basically you need to stop the forward movement of the boat, either before winding up the line (if on your own) or simultaneously with that act (if two anglers on board). I would never myself fish on a slack clutch when using hard baits that can be ejected.

All this is detail which each angler can sort out for himself. What can be guaranteed about waters such as Corrib and Mask is that fishing them for pike is exhilarating, and very variable too – one can be trolling on a big water, or stalking big pike in the reeds along the margins with barely a foot of crystal clear water. It is also quite enjoyable to take a brolly camp outfit and be a backwoodsman, or live on the boat! There is an incomparable atmosphere surrounding these waters, appreciated and encouraged by the locals in a way that doesn't happen in the UK.

Sadly, we still have that strange dichotomy with which I began. It really is not a sensible management policy to kill so many pike now that it is known that they do not, in fact, threaten trout stocks. Removal of pike in the hope of providing a 50 lb plus fish every twenty-five years or so is an untenable argument. Certainly, a great deal is at risk, and not only in tourism terms, if the slaughtering antics of some visiting European nationals are not curtailed. They have badly affected the atmosphere in one or two locales already. All that said, one can avoid hassle in the great loughs of the west so easily. It is still wilderness country.

Boat Fishing for Pike on Large Waters

Boats have been used by rod and line fishermen for thousands of years, yet until recently the basic techniques of hunting and locating fish had changed surprisingly little. However, in the last few years fish-finding techniques have taken a quantum leap, making boat fishing a more attractive prospect than ever before.

Up until a few years ago exploring the underwater contours of an unknown lake or river involved laboriously charting great numbers of plumb line soundings. Now, with the help of modern equipment, fish-holding contours, and even the fish themselves, can be identified on screen and graph paper. The aim of this chapter is to examine the general benefits of boat fishing for pike with particular reference to the practical application of the new techniques now available to the angler.

Firstly, there is no doubt that boats are a great help to fishing on large water, since once afloat the angler is presented with opportunities beyond the scope of the bank-side angler. Neglected islands and weedbeds now come within reach and with the help of an engine one can visit those remote bays which remain unfished by all but the most determined oarsmen. Perhaps one of the greatest advantages of having a boat at one's disposal is being able to pilot those underwater features which are so often haunted by pike. A simple plumb line can be used to locate these underwater shelves and drop-off points, but large waters an echo sounder is a better tool. Not only will it plot underwater features, but it will also indicate the whereabouts of fodder fish, which show up on the screen as tiny intermittent flashes.

The value of using an echo sounder was dramatically illustrated by Fred Wagstaffe and Bob Reynolds when, after several days of moderate sport on Templehouse Lough, an echo sounder was employed successfully to locate the fry shoals. This action led them to catch six pike, together weighing 157 lb, in only twenty-four hours!

The graph recorder is a newly available piece of equipment for the boat angler, and puts the old echo sounder in the shade. The underwater detail shown by the recorder can only be described as staggering and had already been used successfully by many anglers.

Colin Dyson the editor of *Coarse Angler* has more experience than most with the graph recorder and has kindly offered to outline the benefits of using this new equipment.

The Graph Recorder

COLIN DYSON

A bunch of Americans went to a lot of trouble to make sure I got to know about graphs. They included me in a party of journalists invited to Tulsa, Oklahoma, to look around their factory. The home of Lowrance Electronics Inc. was fascinating; using their sophisticated electronic equipment was even more so!

I suppose the difference between the simple depth-finding equipment most British anglers are familiar with and the Lowrance Eagle Mach 1 or X15A, is much the same as the difference between early radio and modern TV. In addition to depth the graphs can show up individual fish and shoals of fish.

A graph is a computerised gadget which, to keep it simple, sends down a 'cone' of sound via transducers which are either fixed to the stern of a boat or set to 'shoot' through the glass hull. The sound bounces back off the bottom, and from anything intervening, and the results are printed out on a paper roll. A fish resting on or near the bottom shows up rather like an inverted tick sign. If it moves while it is within the transducer cone it registers as a smoky mark on the paper – exciting when the boat is trailing maybe eight or ten lures which have been adjusted by downriggers to run at the depths at which the fish are 'marking' on the graph! Several times during the first demonstration on Lake Michigan those smoky marks ended in one of my rods slamming over, and I was into a chinook salmon or a Skamania steelhead. Truly memorable, but what does it all mean for us?

It is an ethical as well as a practical question. In America, where most of the fishing goes on in wide open spaces – often thousands of square miles, like Lake Michigan or the other Great Lakes – the equipment is essential. Over here boat fishing on vast expanses of water is much less frequent a pastime, though anyone interested enough in pike to buy this book will know the exceptions to the rule. Places like Loch Lomond become a much more open book. One of the first rules of pike fishing, finding the prey shoals, becomes a piece of cake. On ethical grounds, I find it hard to condemn equipment which offers the experienced, or

THE GRAPH RECORDER

How it works

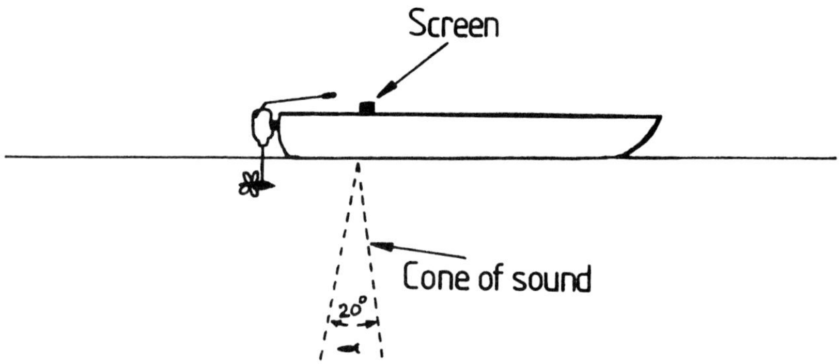

Fish show on the screen as an inverted U

Readout of a gravel pit hotspot X

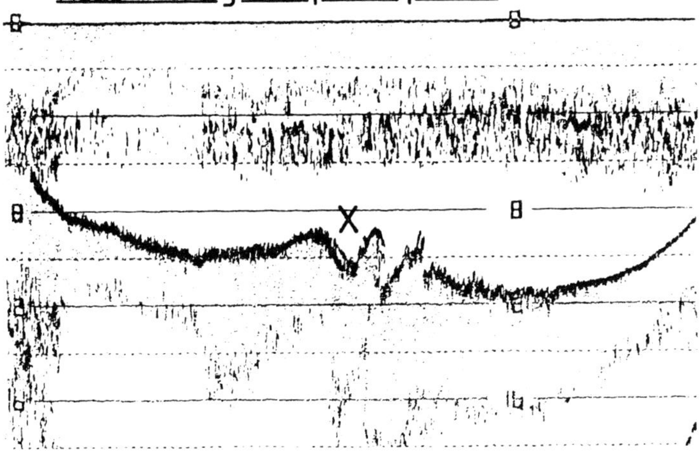

Jetboat collision

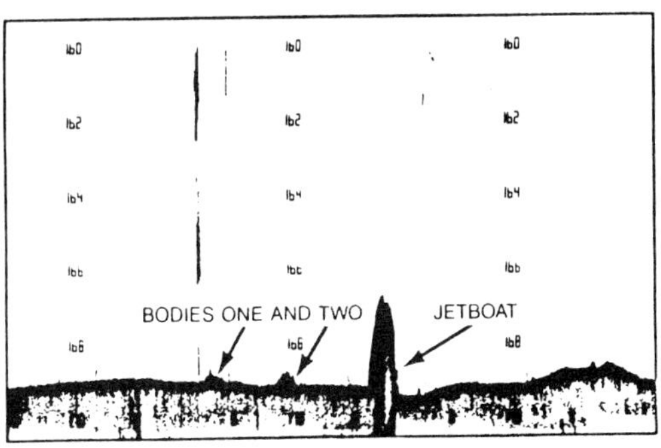

View of jetboat on 10-foot increment of X-15 revealed boat and remains of two victims who perished in collision 18 years earlier.

These two pike were taken whilst the author was fishing on the bank but the swim was located earlier using the Lowrance Eagle equipment. The big fish held by the author weighed 24 lb 8 oz and was taken on Kuusamo professor spoon, the second fish weighed 20 lb 9 oz and fell to livebait. (Photo: C. Dyson)

even inexperienced, angler a short cut to success. The graph tells us little or nothing which we cannot discover by other means; the alternatives just take longer. In four years of fishing a large gravel pit I learned less about it than I did in one day doing a graph survey. I don't feel a bit guilty about it!

It can be a frustrating exercise, though. I am not allowed to fish the pit from the boat, and the likeliest pike holding area I found was way out of reach of the bank. Three large marks, almost certainly pike, were in residence where three deep gullies arrowed towards one meeting point. One of the gullies was stuffed with bream or large hybrids.

Another obvious area could be fished from the bank – a smart drop-off into fifteen feet of water, and then another into twenty feet. The first time I fished them the twenty-foot mark produced a run of fish into double figures. The first run from the fifteen-foot swim came from a pike weighing 21 lb 3 oz.

Large lakes and pits can be weighed up so quickly that the investment – now up to £600 for an Eagle or over £1,000 for the X15A – is well worthwhile for groups of anglers fishing that kind of water. I bought the Eagle, which has all the important functions.

Up to now it has been used more for charting waters than for fish location, but I have few qualms about the latter. My angling time is limited, and I see nothing wrong in using it to the best effect. I see no special merit in clocking up blanks, and the equipment has certainly told me why blanks are so easy to achieve on gravel pits.

Right and wrong spots are often just a few feet apart, and hitting the right spot from the bank is not always easy, even when your charting has been done with great care. Fishing from a boat, however, there is no excuse at all! When the Americans find a likely spot on the graph they throw a marker overboard, and then circle back and anchor within casting distance. The marker is a large, H-shaped polystyrene buoy with rope wrapped around it, terminating in a large lead. The rope unwinds, flipping the marker over and over until the lead hits bottom. They aren't available over here, but would be simple to make.

Fishing where you know the fish are is certainly a confidence booster, though it doesn't guarantee success. 'You can't eat marks on the graph,' is how one American put it, but it's even harder to catch fish which aren't there.

At least one record fish, to my knowledge, has been landed over here after the swim – with large fish in residence – had been located by graph recorder. It may not be the last. Many experienced anglers now either own a graph or a part-share in one. They are getting results, and graph use will increase as a result.

Most of us, though, will never see a record fish, even as a large mark on a graph! We have to settle for less – but even the ordinary is fascinating enough for me. How often have we sat there thinking, 'if only I could really see what's going on down there . . .?' With a graph you actually can, at least in one dimension, and it changes one's whole perception of what goes on. Everyone who has used the equipment says the same.

Pike Fishing in Scottish Waters

BILL WINSHIP

Scotland has always been a place of special interest to the pike angler. The high craggy mountains, vast lochs and endless stories of great pike combine to give Scottish piking a mystical quality which is compulsive to anyone who visits these remote northern waters. Quite recently the legends of big loch pike have been given substance by a number of sportsmen who have taken pike up to and above the 30 lb mark. However, the Scottish lochs, exciting as they may be, are also renowned heart breakers. Authors like Ray Webb and others have warned that these waters present a formidable challenge to even the most experienced loch anglers and there are several reasons why this is so.

Firstly, it is important to recognise that a great deal of Scotland consists of barren mountainous areas. These highlands with their fast rocky streams, acidic peat bogs and cold deep lochs generally fail to provide the productive food chains upon which big pike depend so heavily. When we stop to consider that about 75 per cent of Scotland gives these cold inhospitable conditions we can begin to understand why much of Scotland is not the land of promise it is so often described as. Certainly the sight of a twenty-mile-long loch running to depths of over six hundred feet, bounded by towering mountains, conjures up images of untapped potential. One naturally expects the fish life to reflect the scale and drama of the landscape, yet in reality the opposite is often the case. Many highland lochs simply lack the right conditions for producing monster fish.

Fortunately there are certain lochs which regularly produce pike up to and beyond the 25 lb mark and these are usually the places where the natural background ecology is boosted by an intermittent influx of migratory fish from the sea.

Loch Tay is one such place where sizeable pike are taken regularly by salmon anglers and netsmen. In 1986 a 32 lb specimen pike was taken from the western end by professional netsmen who trap and cull pike annually in an attempt to protect their game fish.

Salmon anglers pay hefty sums of cash to fish loch Tay and yet pike anglers can fish at little or no cost at all. Although most of the pike caught here are killed this does not seem to affect the pike numbers or

MAP TO SHOW SOME OF THE MAIN PIKE LOCHS AND RIVERS IN SCOTLAND

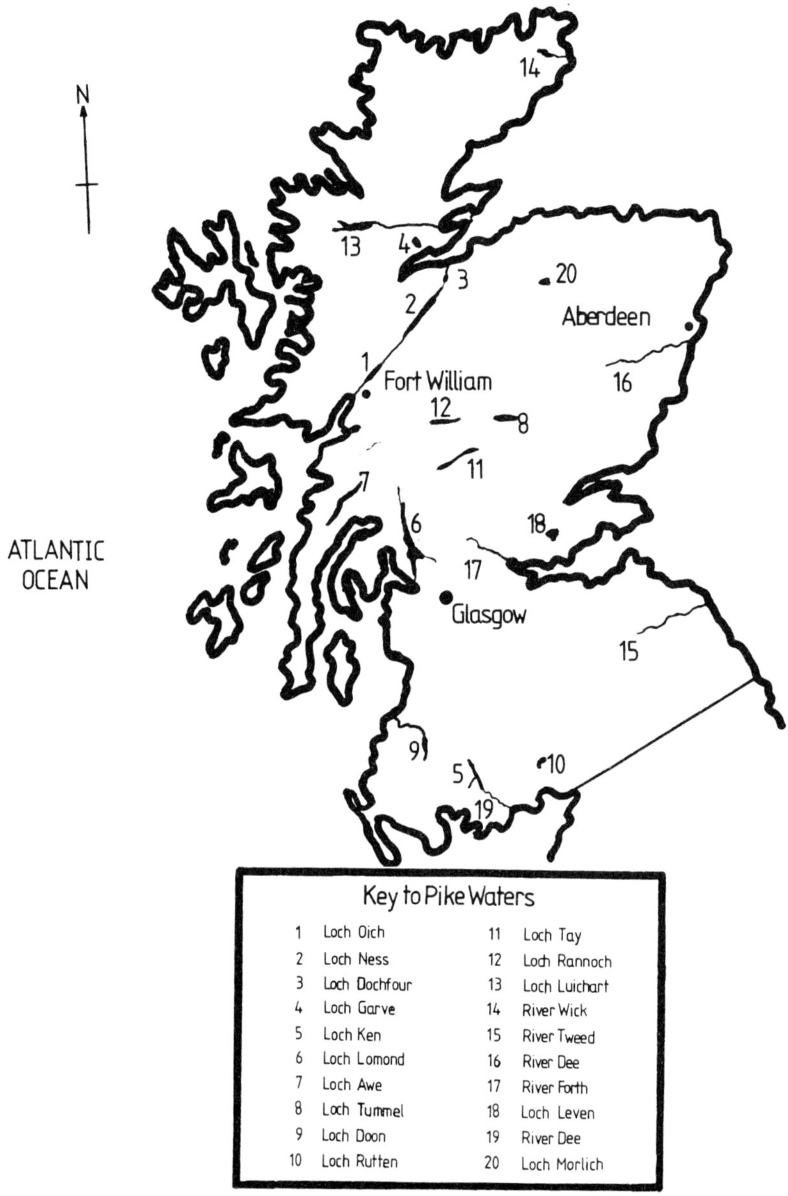

Key to Pike Waters

1	Loch Oich	11	Loch Tay
2	Loch Ness	12	Loch Rannoch
3	Loch Dochfour	13	Loch Luichart
4	Loch Garve	14	River Wick
5	Loch Ken	15	River Tweed
6	Loch Lomond	16	River Dee
7	Loch Awe	17	River Forth
8	Loch Tummel	18	Loch Leven
9	Loch Doon	19	River Dee
10	Loch Rutten	20	Loch Morlich

prevent them from growing to good proportions. With its fine gravel bottom and almost snag-free bed Loch Tay is ideal for trolling from a boat, especially from the western end, which is considered as one of the best areas for pike in springtime.

Loch Ken is another exceptional Scottish pike water which holds pike up to about 30 lb in weight. In the last decade several such fish have been caught by anglers and netsmen from different parts of the loch. The river Dee, which flows out of loch Ken, is also considered to be a good pike water, again producing fish of an unusually high weight for Scotland.

Loch Awe is arguably one of Scotland's most beautiful lochs and though it is set amongst the remote Western Highlands its water temperatures rise a little earlier than those of many other waters, and remain warmer throughout the year. This is due to its proximity to the North Atlantic Drift, which is a 'river' of warm surface water that brings a mild influence to western Scotland from distant tropical oceans to the south. This natural phenomenon, coupled with the seasonal influx of salmon and eels from the sea, provides an ideal habitat for big pike, and fish up to and over 25 lb in weight are taken in most years. Kilchurn Castle, once the stronghold of the famous Campbell family overlooks a number of weedy bays which are known to hold good pike. However it is advisable to get the landowner's permission to fish, especially if overnight sessions are planned.

The lochs so far discussed represent a mere handful of water which provide better than average sport. There are numerous others which are less likely to produce very big pike yet offer wonderful sport in areas of special scenic value. Loch Morlich is one such place. It rests at over a thousand feet above sea level and is dominated by the mountain peaks of the Cairngorms which surround it. Thick coniferous forests run down to the waterside all round the loch and it contains a good head of pike up to about 14 lb in weight with occasional fish up to about 18 lb. In this water the fish are generally on the small side, yet the striking beauty of the surroundings makes it a wonderful place to fish. There are numerous waters in Scotland which support a mixed head of trout, perch and pike in some of the most rugged places possible. Loch Claunie in the Highland Region is an example of a water which supports wild pike and trout in some of the most windswept and barren country in Scotland. Pike and trout seem to make a natural combination in many of these northern waters. They are distributed together as far north as the river Wick near John O' Groats, but the full extent of pike distribution may not be fully realised because owners of game fishing interests naturally keep quiet about their pike stocks for commercial reasons.

Of all the numerous waters available in Scotland it is, of course, Loch Lomond that is the most popular – not least because it was once haunted by Tommy Morgan's 47 lb 'record' pike. However, despite a great deal

Loch Lomond from Duncryne. (Photo: B. Little)

Mountains, deep lochs, and big pike. Three ingredients which give Scottish pike fishing a unique and mystical attraction. (Photo: B. Winship)

This 33 lb Loch Lomond pike is one of the largest pike to have been caught on any of the Scottish lochs. It was taken in spring by the young Dutch boy on the left. It was caught on a small spinner along with several other fish from a shallow weedy bay. (Photo: B. Winship)

of publicity and attention from some noted pike anglers, it has yet to produce anything weighing more than about 35 lb. In view of the fact that Loch Lomond is recognised as Scotland's premier pike water, and considering the amount of attention it has received, one cannot help but conclude that its big fish potential is less than that of the premier English waters, which are now producing fish in excess of 40 lb almost every year. However there is a lot more to the sport of pike fishing than hunting record-breaking specimens; for those who are content to fish with a realistic chance of a thirty pounder there can be few places more pleasant than Loch Lomond.

The dramatic scale of the Scottish lochs came about over twelve thousand years ago when a series of glaciers (frozen rivers) scoured out deep trenches in the valley floor. Some valleys were deepened so much that they later became flooded by the sea (Loch Long for instance). Others, like Loch Lomond, were inundated with fresh water but remain so deep that great areas remain barren and infertile. It is the sheer scale, coupled with the relative barrenness, of the Scottish lochs that makes them difficult to fish. Back in fertile England one may expect to find a 20 lb pike in every five of ten acres of water. However, on a water like Lomond, the whole scale range is different. Here there may be only one 20 lb pike for every thousand acres. It is this difference in scale that confounds so many visitors from England. Big loch pike have seasonal movement and behaviour patterns which, fortunately, can be predicted almost as easily as on the smaller and more intimate waters. However, the sheer scale of these waters enhances the importance of locating the pike. On a water which is twenty miles long and several miles wide it is much easier to fish in the wrong place than on a ten acre gravel pit. Location is the key. Because of its importance the following chapter will deal in detail with the subject of pike location. The chapter is written by Bill Little who has made an informal study of the problems of pike location on Scottish lochs.

Catching Pike from Scottish Lochs

BILL LITTLE

In recent years there has been a tremendous increase in the interest shown in Scottish loch piking. Unfortunately, most of this interest centres around springtime fishing when the pike congregate on the shallows to spawn. This is a pity because although sport can be quite good during this period, it is often better at other times of the year.

The real peak period for Scottish piking is between June and November when the fish are at their fighting best. This is the time of the year when mobility and versatility will bring rewards. Gone for another year is the shoulder to shoulder, static style of fishing which is practised in the shallow, weedy bays in spring. Now is the time to take to the boats, get out on the wide open spaces of the loch and discover what Scottish loch piking is all about.

Winter fishing can also be productive but at this time of year the lochs need to be treated with even greater respect than normal. Weather conditions can change unbelievably quickly in winter and even the most experienced loch piker can get caught out. Last winter, two mates and myself found ourselves 'snowed in' for twenty-four hours in a remote area of one of the bigger lochs when a severe blizzard struck unexpectedly. Fortunately we were, as usual, very well equipped to handle such weather and were never in any real danger. In actual fact we were so well prepared that we were able to bank fish during the worst of the blizzard and to catch a few fish as well.

Yes, Scottish piking is truly an all year round pursuit but the fishing is not easy and success can only be achieved once the basic problem of location has been overcome. To many newcomers this appears to represent some sort of insurmountable obstacle as they allow themselves to be overawed by the sheer size of some of these waters. Fortunately there are short cuts which can be taken to reduce waters to more manageable proportions.

J. Moran and Bill Little with a brace of loch pike. (Photo: B. Little)

PREPARATION

On a loch which could measure up to twenty miles long and be several miles wide, it makes sense to try to find out a bit about it before actually fishing it. The simplest way to do this is to produce an accurate and detailed hydrographic chart of the chosen water. On Lomond this task is made slightly easier, at least initially, by the production of an Admiralty Chart (No. 2021) but even this seemingly detailed chart is not as accurate as it appears to be. The original survey was carried out in 1861 and a lot will have changed since then due to such things as silting up, particularly around river mouths.

On other lochs, where an Admiralty Chart is not available, a 1:50,000 or, better still, a 1:25,000 scale Ordnance Survey map can form the basis of the chart. This OS map will already show simplified depth contours of the larger lochs, and further information about the general configuration of the bottom can be obtained by studying the contours of the surrounding land.

The first step in the process of turning this simple contour map into a practical fish-finding chart is to blank out all areas where the water is deeper than 50 feet (15 metres). This step has the effect of reducing the area of water we need concern ourselves with, in normal circumstances. On big waters such as Lomond, Awe and Tay this will reduce the area by about 80 per cent obviously on some of the smaller waters this figure will be a great deal less or even none at all. I should point out that when

I originally selected 50 feet I did so for no real reason, but my choice would appear to be justified as I have never taken a pike from deeper than 43 feet. This now leaves a map which clearly shows the amount of fishable water on the loch.

The next stage is to break the loch up into small easily defined areas which can then be treated as individual lakes. Always try to include an obvious feature such as a headland, island, river mouth or bay in each area (or lake) as they generally make good starting points.

Now that the initial groundwork has been done and a few likely spots noted, it is time to get out on the loch. A word of caution though: the map which has been prepared so far is still a very sketchy affair with very little reliable or useful detail. To turn this map into a more useful tool a lot more detail will have to be added and, realistically, this can only be done by employing an echo sounder.

At this juncture I don't intend to go into echo sounders in any detail as this subject has been dealt with 'in depth' by Colin Dyson in a previous chapter. For anyone who is keen to try loch fishing a 'pinger' is an absolute necessity and Colin's chapter will be of special interest.

When surveying an area don't try to deal with too big an area at once; work in a methodical manner using a compass. By following compass bearings from fixed starting points and noting irregularities such as drop-offs, ledges, gullies and gravel bars, you soon build up a comprehensive picture of the bottom. At this stage don't ignore anything as every little feature on the bottom is a potential fish holding spot.

This may seem like a lot of hard work just to locate a few fish, especially to those anglers who only fish the known hot spots on Lomond and Awe. The methods I am describing, however, are meant to help the angler who wants to fish other waters where the productive areas are not so well known. They will also help the angler who fishes the well known waters but who wants to get away from the 'madding crowd' and find new areas. In these situations a couple of hours spent with an echo sounder and map can be worth several days fishing blind. However, it should not be assumed that, because time has been taken to produce a pukka chart, success is guaranteed. The chart is only as good as the angler's ability to relate the features on it to the preferred habitat of the pike themselves.

HABITAT

One of the main attractions of loch fishing, apart from the pike themselves, is the rich variety of locations from which they can be caught. Here we have a fish which is not bound by any severe limitation of environment as is often the case on smaller, shallow waters. On a big loch the pike have a tremendous choice of places to live and feed.

Bill Little with the 21 lb 14 oz pike mentioned in the text. (Photo: B. Little)

It is because of this choice that the bigger fish have, perhaps surprisingly to some people, turned their backs on those much loved pikey hot spots, the shallow weed beds. That they do visit these weedy areas in spring to spawn is undoubtedly true but outside this period the bigger fish are seldom found there. The reason for this is quite simple. They don't live there. These weed beds do, however, provide a haven for large numbers of jack pike, and just occasionally a big fish will cruise by in the hope of a decent-sized meal. So although it doesn't pay to write off these weed beds completely, they are not permanent holders of big fish. No, the place to find these big wild fish is down amongst the boulders, sunken trees and snag-ridden drop-offs in the deeper water.

Scottish lochs by the very nature of their creation are very well provided with this type of habitat, their rocky bottoms being covered with huge jumbled piles of boulders which were deposited there when the glaciers melted thousands of year ago. Since then millions of tons of sand, gravel and debris have been washed into the loch, by countless winter floods, to form extensive areas of sandbanks and gravel bars with a liberal sprinkling of snags. A pike just couldn't ask for a better environment in which to live and hunt.

So what are the qualities that make these gullies, ledges and drop-offs so appealing to pike? Obviously food supply is a factor but so too is the provision of cover from which prey can be ambushed. In most instances the cover is provided by the blackness of the deeper water, just over the edge. This, combined with the way in which the bunched contours form a bottleneck to fish movements, makes such features ideal spots for 'old *esox*' to strike upwards at the silhouetted prey fish.

Although the majority of loch piking will be carried out at the very edge of these drop-offs, the shallow water on top can at certain times produce some very good fish. The pike seemingly spend most of the day down in the deeper water but in the evening they come onto the shallows to hunt. This time also coincides with an increase in the activity of trout, eels and, on Lomond, powan. After spending the hours of darkness on the shallows the pike then drop back into deeper water some time around dawn.

This particular aspect of pike behaviour was first brought home to me one morning when I was fishing a very steep drop-off. I had livebaits set at between 14 and 25 feet but sport had been very quiet with only one fish, a thirteen pounder, being taken from about 18 feet. I decided to try a bait on the boulder strewn shallows behind the boat and so I set the float at 2 feet and cast out. I have to admit that it did look a little strange, seeing a float bobbing about in amongst all that rock, but I certainly wasn't complaining ten minutes later when I landed a fish of 21 lb 14 oz. The most interesting thing about that particular pike was that, although it took in 2 feet of water, the manner of the take suggested that the fish was coming off the shallows and dropping into the depths.

That fish also demonstrated to me that, when the fish are not in their usual haunts on the drop-off, it pays to experiment with different approaches. Cast a bait under the overhanging bushes along the shoreline, or in amongst the boulders, or even amongst the trees if the loch has flooded. I have and it has produced some memorable fish for me.

Now we know a little bit about where the pike prefer to live but what does it prefer to eat?

PIKE FOOD (NATURAL)

Much has been written in the past about the relationship between migratory fish and big pike. Personally I don't think they contribute a great deal to the diet of loch pike because the runs are too irregular to be a dependable source of food. In fact there are numerous waters in Scotland which have produced 30 lb plus fish and which don't get runs of migratory fish. This is not to suggest that migratory fish are never eaten by pike; of course they are, but not in any significant numbers. Pike are not stupid creatures – they wouldn't have survived for thirty million years if they were; they will eat the food which is most common and easiest to obtain in any water.

On many lochs this will probably be perch, roach, eels and brown trout, but Lomond powan are a major factor. Any fish which swim around in shoals, which at times can cover an area the size of a football pitch, are not to be ignored. Perch were once very common on Lomond but at present they seem to have succumbed to disease and have become very thin on the ground. On some other lochs char will probably feature prominently on the pikes 'menu' but, this is something outside my own experience. I won't speculate further.

Don't underestimate the importance of eels as pikefodder; these lochs can be absolutely heaving with them in summer. It seems certain that they will form a major part of a pikes diet as they are plentiful, easy to catch and a good-sized meal. The number of big fish being taken on eel section nowadays would appear to lend weight to this view.

Cannibalism also appears to be a common practice among loch pike, judging by the number of times I've had pike grabbed when I've been playing them. Of course it could be that the struggles of the smaller fish trigger off an instinctive attack, but I don't think so. It has been a long held theory of mine that the really huge pike in these lochs feed almost exclusively on jack pike. A jack pike provides a large easily-caught meal which is exactly what an exceptionally large pike would be looking for. Spending most of their time in the 25 to 40 foot depth band, these bruisers only come within range of the majority of pike anglers while on one of their infrequent visits to shallower water on a 'grab a jack' mission. The only way to put this theory to the test would be to fish exclusively with jacks for a couple of seasons but, unfortunately, I have never been able to obtain a good enough supply to put this into practice.

My conviction about this 'large pike eating smaller pike' theory has been further strengthened by two incidents in the last couple of years. On both occasions I was playing medium-sized pike when they were grabbed by unseen monsters. These huge fish hung on for several minutes before letting go, leaving me to reel in the chewed up remains of my original fish. The smallest of these mangled pike weighed 7 lb 3 oz and the other was a double! The sceptics are probably thinking this sounds like another fisherman's tale but both incidents occurred in front of witnesses. How big these fish were I'll never know but they have certainly reinforced my belief in the legendary pike of bygone days.

A phenomenon I have encountered on Lomond, particularly in early summer, is the massing of huge shoals of sticklebacks at the edge of deep water. I have no idea why thousands of these little fish should do this, but they do and they are indicated by dimpling on the surface. I first encountered this strange behaviour a few years back when fishing with a mate. He cast a livebait into the middle of a huge shoal and the float didn't even settle – it just shot under. The pike weighed 13 lb 12 oz and whilst being boated it coughed up a load of sticklebacks. The same thing has now happened on several separate occasions, and so it shouldn't be ignored. I don't think it would be possible to 'bag-up' in

Bill Little plays a big pike. Tackle has to be strong to keep fish out of the snags. (Photo: B. Little)

these situations but they do produce an occasional good fish.

Try to put yourself in the position of the pike. Look for the most reliable and easily obtained food source in your chosen water, but be prepared to alter your approach to suit any localised change. Whether it is a run of sea trout, a passing shoal of powan, kelts dropping back from a spawning stream or an influx of elvers, don't turn a blind eye, because *esox* certainly won't.

PIKE BAITS

Over the years I've kept a record of all the fish my mates and I have caught and the baits used and I've concluded that no single bait stands out as being particularly productive. My records show that one third of our fish took trout livebaits, one third took coarse livebaits and the other third were split between sea baits, coarse deadbaits, trout deadbaits and lures. At first glance this would seem to suggest that livebaits are twice as likely to produce a fish as other methods, but this is incorrect. The fact is that we tend to fish livebaits twice as often as deadbaits and lures, which roughly corresponds with the results achieved.

Our choice of livebaits is limited only by availability and not by any preference of the pike. As trout and roach are easiest for us to obtain, it is no surprise that they tend to predominate in our catch records. Other species have been used from time to time with no noticeable difference in results.

With deadbaits we have tended to be a bit more selective, preferring to stick mainly to trout and sea baits, coarse baits being a very poor third choice. With all of them, however, the most important factor is that they be absolutely fresh when frozen. We now consider this to be of such importance that we prefer to catch our own mackerel, just to be sure of its freshness. This ultra-fresh mackerel consistently outfishes shop-bought bait and, while it hasn't produced many large bags of fish, it had certainly sorted out some heavyweights. Sardines, herrings, sprats and smelts have all produced their share of fish, but for the bigger fish they don't come close to fresh mackerel.

To my mind, however, bait selection is not a critical consideration other than it should be of the best quality possible. Much more important is the ability to present that bait in the right place at the right time.

TACKLE AND TECHNIQUES

By virtue of the terrain in which loch pike live it is fairly obvious that tackle needs to be on the heavy side. Rods should be in the 2½–3½ lb TC range and lines should never be less than 15 lb bs I now tend to use 18 lb bs for most of my loch piking but have on occcasion gone up to 26 lb bs in extremely snaggy situations. This may appear to be a rather extreme measure but it is a lot better than having broken-up tackle and leaving a set of hooks in a fish.

I've never subscribed to the view that multipliers are essential when fishing for loch pike. I've fished for them now for fourteen years and caught some very big pike when using standard fixed spools. I own several multipliers, being a converted sea angler, but I still prefer to use fixed spools as they allow me to backwind on a fish. In the snaggy conditions found on many lochs it is often necessary to give line very grudgingly and the most efficient way to do this is to backwind.

Hooks, wire and swivels should be of the best quality available because sometimes it is necessary to hold fish very hard when in amongst the boulders and snags. In such a situation any weakness will soon be made apparent in fairly dramatic fashion.

All the standard methods of bait presentation work on the lochs but in certain types of location some methods appear to be more suitable than others. From a boat in water up to 15 feet deep and with a clean bottom I would use a float leger, float paternoster, suspended or drifted bait. However, in snaggy conditions or deeper water the bait would be either suspended or paternostered to keep it clear of any debris found on the bottom. All the rigs I now use are deliberately kept very simple

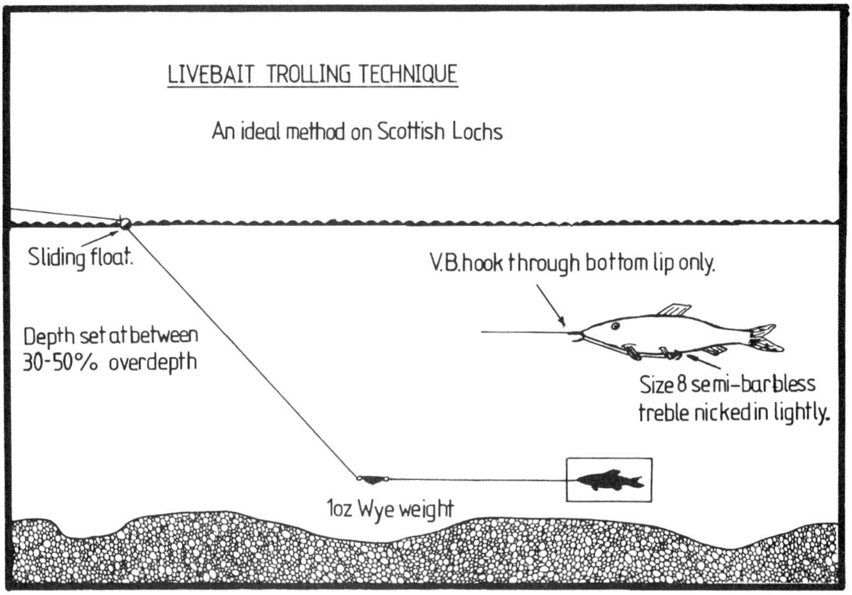

to minimise the chances of tangling, especially when fishing in deep water.

A typical day afloat would begin before dawn with the boat anchored up in an area where the bottom drops away steeply into deeper water. At this time I would have two baits, one livebait and one deadbait, on the shallow shelf and another livebait paternostered in 15 feet of water. As the morning progressed I would move the shallow-fished livebait into much deeper water which could be up to 30 to 35 feet deep. The deadbait would always remain in the shallow water in normal conditions. If nothing was forthcoming by about mid-morning I would up-anchor and move to a completely new area.

If, however, I felt strongly enough that there were pike in the area, I would row around and float troll livebaits. I've lost count of the number of times I've been sitting for hours without a run to conventional methods, then, within minutes of starting to float troll, I've had a take. I always row at a nice gentle pace following a set contour using the echo sounder, this slow pace allowing the pike maximum time to see and attack the bait. Trolling livebaits is one method where a good, detailed chart of the loch is advantageous, as it is a great deal easier to follow a given contour when you know exactly what is coming up in front of the boat. This is a method which can also be used to search out new holding areas; just troll around until a fish takes then anchor up and fish the area in the normal way. You never know, you might just get a pleasant surprise.

As evening approached I would go back to a known mark and sit

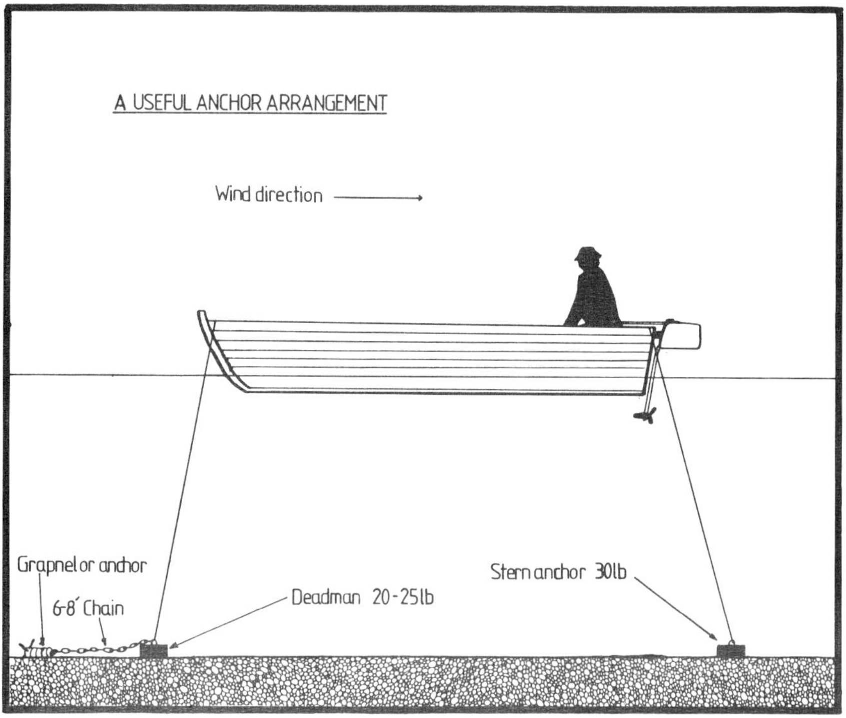

it out until after dark. I would begin with livebaits set at between 15 and 25 feet, and with a deadbait on the shallow ledge, but as darkness started to fall I'd gradually move the deepest livebait up into the shallower water until it was positioned on the very edge of the drop-off. This would ensure that at least one bait was in the right position to intercept any pike moving up onto the shallows.

Once total darkness has fallen it is time to up-anchor and make my way back to base. As this can sometimes entail a journey of up to five miles across the loch it makes me appreciate all the hours spent studying charts. For many visiting anglers a trip to a Scottish loch may well be the first time they have to fish from a boat, in which case navigating after dark should not be attempted. There are more than enough problems to be faced and overcome, even during daylight. It is as well to remember that there is no fish that swims for which is worth risking your life.

BOAT FISHING AND SAFETY AFLOAT

When boat fishing it is absolutely vital that everthing should be well organised. All spare tackle should be neatly stored away and remain that way during the course of the day. Fishing from a small boat is uncomfortable at the best of times but an untidy boat can make it almost unbearable – and extremely dangerous.

An area of the boats, preferably amidships, should be kept clear as an unhooking area for any pike caught. This area should also be covered with a soft material, such as carpet underlay, to protect the fish.

When travelling about the loch the rods should, if possible, be laid neatly inside the boat with the tips pointing towards the bow. Take care not to tangle any of the lines or traces; I have seen some wonderful acrobatic displays on boats where this has been allowed to happen. When actually fishing, the rods will be in rests which hold most of the rod outside the boat, thus creating more space.

Livebaits are kept in a plastic bucket which is hung over the side of the boat when fishing. The top of the bucket can be perforated to allow water circulation, but the method I prefer is to remove the lid altogether and replace it with a piece of netting secured by a piece of elasticated rope. Keepnets are not recommended because it is still necessary to carry a bucket in which to put the baits while travelling between fishing spots.

The biggest single item that has to be stowed onboard is the landing net. Fortunately, when fishing with a partner the handle is not needed, which saves a bit of space especially if the net can be folded away when not in use. The solo angler must use the handle, but as the space problem is not so critical the situation balances itself out.

To fish efficiently it is essential that the boat be positioned exactly where you want it and held there. Over the years I have tried various methods of anchoring, including the ubiquitous 56 lb weight, but I hadn't found a completely satisfactory system until recently. For this method I will be forever grateful to Roger Hatcher, who is certainly no stranger to the larger residents of Loch Lomond.

The principal behind this anchoring system (see diagram) is that on the rare occasions when there is practically no wind, the boat is held stationary by the weight on the bottom. As the wind increases, the vertical motion of the boat lifts the deadman and some of the chain. The boat, however, remains stationary due to the increasing weight of the chain and the inability of the grapnel to move because of the horizontal distance between it and the deadman. If the boat insists on moving when this system is in use then it is time to pack up and go home as quickly as possible.

All of which brings me nicely to the weather conditions which can be experienced on a big Scottish loch. It is no joke to say that it is possible to experience all the four seasons in a single day. An idyllic, glassy calm loch can be transformed into a maelstrom of white foaming waves in a remarkably short space of time. Always check the weather forecast before venturing out and heed the advice of the locals. If a sudden storm does blow up and you don't fancy trying to get back to base, head for the nearest shore, pull the boat up and sit it out. Quite often these sudden vicious squalls are of short duration and it is possible to make your way home in safety without having to wait too long. Even if the storm doesn't pass quickly and it is necessary to spend the night there, that is a lot safer than trying to run for it. It may be a cold and miserable night but at least you won't drown on dry land.

In all forms of angling it is essential to keep warm and dry, but when fishing from a boat this can at times be difficult to achieve. If you get cold when fishing from the bank you can always wander up and down, or if it rains you can sit under a brolly, but you can't do either of these things in a 16 foot boat. Your only protection from the elements is your clothing and a constant intake of warm food, such as soup. As far as clothing is concerned I have yet to find any form of waterproof which is 100 per cent effective. No matter how expensive or seemingly well designed a garment is the rain always seems to find a way in. The best that can be done is to minimise the amount which gets through.

Warm soup or coffee from a flask can be a godsend, but freshly brewed beverages always seem to be that little bit better. A small portable stove is a good idea – but always go ashore before lighting up. Fuel from outboard motors has a nasty habit of leaking; being warm is preferable to third degree burns. Anyway a spell ashore can be quite therapeutic as it allows you to loosen stiff joints, warm up and generally revitalise yourself for a return to the fray.

As it is well known that if something can go wrong then it probably will, it is as well to be prepared for it. I always carry some basic safety equipment so that in the event of an emergency I am able to handle it. It goes without saying that a life-jacket or buoyancy aid should be carried, but so too should a compass. It is always reassuring to know in which direction safety lies if a real pea-souper of a fog comes down. I have been caught out once before and I don't intend to be caught again. A good torch and waterproof matches come in handy if the weather turns really nasty and you have to spend a night on an island or remote shore. A small tool kit, spare spark plug(s) for the outboard and a first-aid kit complete the emergency equipment.

Of course, with a little common sense and forethought most emergencies can be avoided, but it's nice to know that you can deal with any should the need arise. This leaves you free to enjoy your fishing and soak up that special atmosphere which is unique to the Scottish lochs.

IN CONCLUSION

These days pike fishing for me is all about enjoyment and I consider myself very fortunate to be able to pursue my sport amongst some of the most breathtaking countryside in Britain. When you fish these waters regularly you quickly learn to appreciate your surroundings so that even blank days can be memorable. How can a blank day be considered a failure when you have seen a white fallow deer buck or witnessed the spectacular courtship display of a cock capercaillie. I can even remember a day when seven anglers, myself included, all blanked and not one of us felt dejected – quite the opposite. The reason for our elation was that we had been privileged to see one of the most spectacular ornithological dogfights of all time. In the sky at the one time there were two buzzards, two golden eagles and two peregrine falcons all doing battle for the right to hunt on that particular area of lochside. Over the years, by my reckoning, I may have had plenty of blank sessions but I certainly haven't had many failures.

Then there are those days which don't require any help from the animal or bird kingdom to make them memorable – those days when *lucius* is about in numbers and feeding as if there were no tomorrow. One such day occurred in October a couple of years back when two mates and myself found a pack of large hungry predators in the lee of a small rocky headland during a storm. What those fish were doing packed tightly in such a small shallow area I don't know; perhaps they were sheltering from the storm as well. Whatever the reason, they were feeding like mad and in the space of about an hour we took seven good fish with the best three going over 20 lb. They weighed 21 lb 6 oz, 23 lb 4 oz and 28 lb 12 oz, and the largest of them, which fell to my rod, literally towed the boat around for twenty odd minutes before being netted. What made this day especially memorable for me was the fact that the twenties were nicely split up with each of us getting one apiece.

Leaving memories of the past aside, what does the future hold for the loch piker? With more and more pike anglers putting more and more baits into the lochs it would seem that the possibility of a monster pike turning up is greater. I now feel, however, that if a huge pike is going to turn up it will probably do so in winter when there are fewer anglers about, but they tend to concentrate on deeper water. This is a view which is shared by quite a few of the loch regulars.

There is no doubt that lure fishing will play an increasing role in the loch fishing scene in the next few years as more and more lures become available. New methods of presentation (new to this country at any rate), such as the downrigger, will become more common and allow lures to be fished at greater depths, hence making lure fishing even more versatile.

Relations with game anglers have been improving slowly over the past few years, so much so that some of the more enlightened ones are now putting pike back alive. Unfortunately there are a lot of waters where the old ways are still practised, and pike culling is very much the order of the day. It would be extremely naïve to believe that, in a country where salmon and trout are regarded as the only rightful occupants of any water, things will change appreciably. The one area that is proving contentious and threatening to destroy all the goodwill that has been built up is the illegal dumping of unused livebaits in the lochs by visiting anglers. This practise must be stopped immediately if we are not to suffer the consequences, as has happened in Ireland.

Finally, I return to the subject of the existence of monster pike in the Scottish lochs. During the mid-seventies I had the privilege of corresponding with the late Richard Walker on the subject of Loch Lomond and its pike fishing. This was around the time of the great controversy about the record-breaking potential of Lomond and the other Scottish lochs. In his final letter to me he finished with the line 'So go catch me a fifty pounder and prove me right and all the "doubting Thomases" wrong.' Well I'm still trying and I'm enjoying every minute of it.

Pike in Reservoirs and Gravel Pits

MARTIN GAY

Over the past decade an interesting fact has emerged from the management of pike fisheries, particularly trout reservoirs – a fact which causes a division in the ideas of many pike anglers. It all has to do with the culling, or otherwise, of the pike stocks and the resulting effects on the growth rate of the remaining pike. In a quality water containing good coarse fish stocks and a regular injection of trout, pike can exist almost unnoticed and grow to a prodigious size. In such circumstances, with very few pike being caught, and despite the quality of the food available to them, it sometimes proves to be the case that they easily control their own numbers, never becoming a nuisance to the trout angler, and thereby holding off any call for culling.

With a low stock density of pike a higher than average number of fish grow to a large size. In angling terms it is difficult to achieve regular success on such fisheries, but they are in demand by sheer virtue of the large average size of the (relatively) few pike usually landed. A second scenario, and one which is perhaps more common, occurs when there is a pike 'explosion' early in the history of a reservoir. This often results in regular pike culling exercises with well documented and predictable results. Netting operations, as a rule, tend to find the mature pike – say fish upwards of six pounds, those very fish which self-predate thereby keeping down the numbers of one- and two-year class pikelets. Removal of these larger predators enables increased numbers of young pike to grow through the prolific period until they reach the size at which they themselves are most likely to be netted!

The annual netting of reservoirs, particularly in the spring, can be very efficient in clearly defined areas. Over a period of several years the result of intense removal of the larger pike is almost always a reduction in the average weight of the remaining pike, but an increase in the total numbers. It is at this point in the scheme of things that an interesting fact emerges. No matter how successful pike removal programmes aim to be, a few pike always manage to avoid the nets and, with the additional food thereby available to them (namely the hordes of young pike), they

A nice solid pike taken on paternostered livebait. (Photo: M. Gay)

grow to a considerable size, sometimes larger than their counterparts in 'untouched' fisheries.

These big pike are often very fast growing, but there is a strong feeling amongst some pike anglers that these same fish do not live as long as the slower-growing fish in more normal situations. This culling situation, if correctly analysed, may lead to a more noticeable, and more rapid, decline in the productivity of the fishing simply because there are fewer back-up pike of a size to interest most pike anglers.

Probably as a result of the continuous replacement of water supplies to a reservoir, the quality of the water is invariably high, clear and fertile. Fish produce what are called anti-metabolites, which limit growth in contained water. This is precisely why fish in small aquariums rarely grow to more than a few inches in length; but frequent, even daily, water changing will result in those same fish growing to at least half the length of the container. Obviously in a natural environment with continuous water changing such problems do not occur and the fish grow to a large size. It is this size of pike which attracts many pike anglers to reservoirs.

This may be an opportune time to lay one misunderstanding. It is often quoted that pike in (certain) reservoirs, and lochs, grow big because of the diet of game fish. This is not the reason, nor always the result. Where trout and, to a lesser extent, salmon are present they are of course preyed upon by the pike, but in every case the common prey-fish will be the main target for the pike. It is these same coarse fish that provide the bulk of the growth potential of the pike; the trout merely add a bonus, though a highly nutritional one, to the pikes' staple diet. I strongly suspect that the abnormal girths frequently found on trout-reservoir pike (not loch pike though) and trout-fishery pike are caused by the highly nutritious oils contained within trout flesh. In many modern reservoirs on which trout fishing is available, the frequent stockings of trout provide a regular bonus to the pikes' food intake, but they are not the main diet.

Apart from in rare instances it is not financially viable to create *small* public water-supply reservoirs. Consequently, public water-supply reservoirs are often several hundred acres in size. This immediately presents pike location problems which often keep all but diehard pike anglers away. The relative peace, the available space and problems therein, are equally the reasons why many of us enjoy fishing these places so much and spend many a miserable winter's day on them!

Fortunately, however, the location of pike is not always that difficult and even on the most barren of reservoirs there are always some pointers. Reservoirs are not filled up by natural seepage as this would be far too unpredictable and unreliable to ensure a good supply to our

Not all reservoirs are concrete bowls! (Photo: M. Gay)

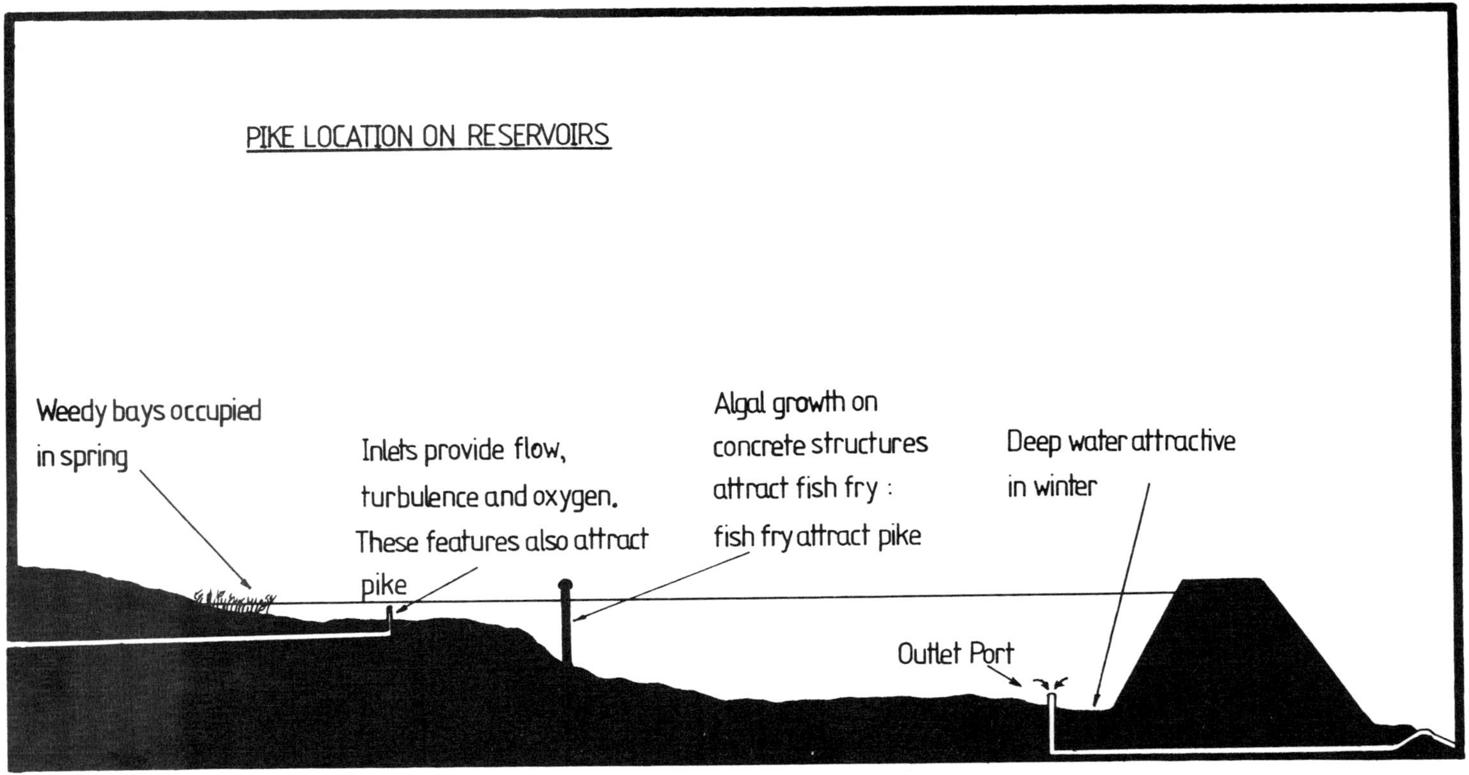
PIKE LOCATION ON RESERVOIRS
Weedy bays occupied in spring
Inlets provide flow, turbulence and oxygen. These features also attract pike
Algal growth on concrete structures attract fish fry : fish fry attract pike
Deep water attractive in winter
Outlet Port

large towns. Water is either pumped in or fed via a local stream or river. On the King George V reservoirs at Chingford, for example, water is pumped because the reservoir is actually above ground level. Abberton reservoir near Colchester is topped up by a natural stream and is pump-fed from the river Stour. Ardingley reservoir in Sussex is supplied by a natural stream. Such are just three examples of reservoirs which all have the same things in common: an inflow of water, water turbulence, and disturbance, and an oxygen source. All these things will attract fry and other food fish which in turn attract pike. Similarly, water is extracted and in the same way this disturbance, which creates a flow, attracts the prey fish. Water is extracted in a number of ways but usually via a valve tower or pumping station. In addition to this artificially created water flow the valve tower, or pump house, which is built actually 'on' the water, is a structure in itself, a fish attractor. Algae grows on the concrete, fry feed on algae, pike feed on the fry. It is most unusual for there not to be some pike almost permanently resident near the valve tower and near the inflow stream. Both are good starting points.

One feature which even so-called natural reservoirs have and which distinguishes them from gravel pits or lakes, is the dam wall. Any valley (or raised structure in some cases) which is subsequently flooded must have a dam and invariably, though not always, the deepest water is found not far away; it may even be directly off the dam wall itself. Quite often this deep water is actually deeper than the fish prefer, but in winter such an environment affords a degree of temperature an disturbance stability which is attractive. Again, the dam wall forms a structure which attracts grazing fish, which in turn attract pike. Above all else, on these big waters always (except at the approach of the breeding season) look for places which will attract the prey fish and the pike will not be far away.

Occasionally the water is artificially aerated and, in a few cases, actually extracted via 'ports' which are located well out from the shore and in deep water. The amount of turbulence thus created is quite considerable and, judging from the number of grebes and comorants continuously feeding around them these areas must attract an awful lot of small fish, and pike.

Most reservoirs, and certainly those with 'natural' banks, will have shallow areas, sometimes encroached by trees and rushes. These are usually the areas favoured by the pike for spawning. As a guideline only, such areas will show a steady build up of pike numbers from January; one pointer to such gatherings is the dispersal of pike around Christmas time from previously reliable hotspots. On entirely man-made reservoirs such obvious spawning sites may not be present. Although it is difficult to be certain in all cases, the weeded concrete slopes in the lee of the prevailing wind, and the vicinity of culverts are

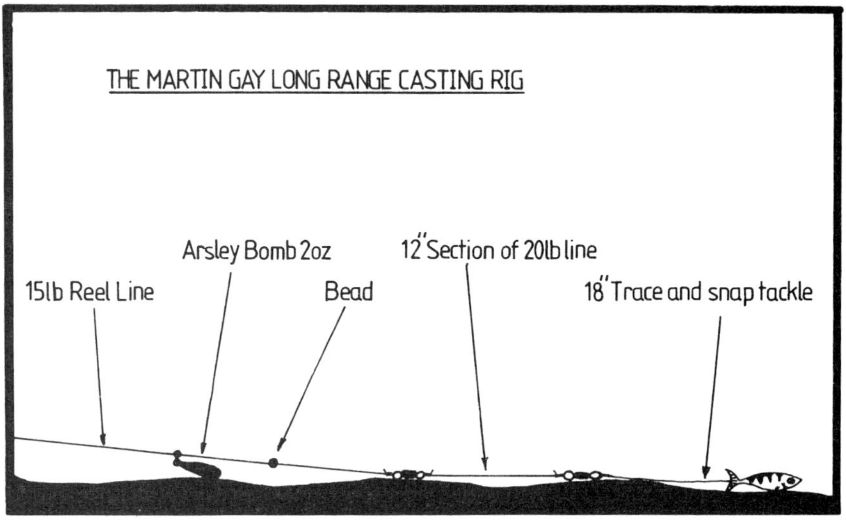

the likely spawning sites. Unfortunately, however, you may not witness such activity because the water is likely to be deep. Pike may prefer shallow, rapidly warmed water in which to spawn but they do very well in deep water if they have to, although the absolute spawning success is rather less in such cases.

Culverts bringing oxygenated water into the reservoir valve towers and pumping stations are normally within easy casting range of the bank, though equally they often run into deep water and may demand specialised or adapted techniques. Long-range legering usually causes the biggest problem with terminal tackle (especially baited hooks) tangle with the main line. This is caused by the bait, which is lighter in weight than the heavy lead needed to achieve the range being cast, flowing backwards, either during the cast or more commonly as the tackle sinks through the water, and tangling with the line. A 'bite off' almost always results! One of the modern anti-tangle booms may be used, of course, but I personally don't find them as effective as the manufacturers claim. A far simpler and cast-free system can be used and is described as follows.

Attach an Arsley bomb to a link swivel and slide that up the reel line. Follow it with a bead, then tie a number 10 or 12 swivel to the end of the reel line. To this swivel tie 12 inches of line 5 lb bs greater (and thus stiffer) than the reel line and thereafter attach your trace swivel to the other end of this short length of line.

You may find you do more legering on reservoirs than you do normally, though there is no reason whatever why you shouldn't float fish a free-swimming livebait, paternoster a live- or deadbait, or vane-float drift a bait to the horizon.

In some cases a change of technique will score heavily, especially if

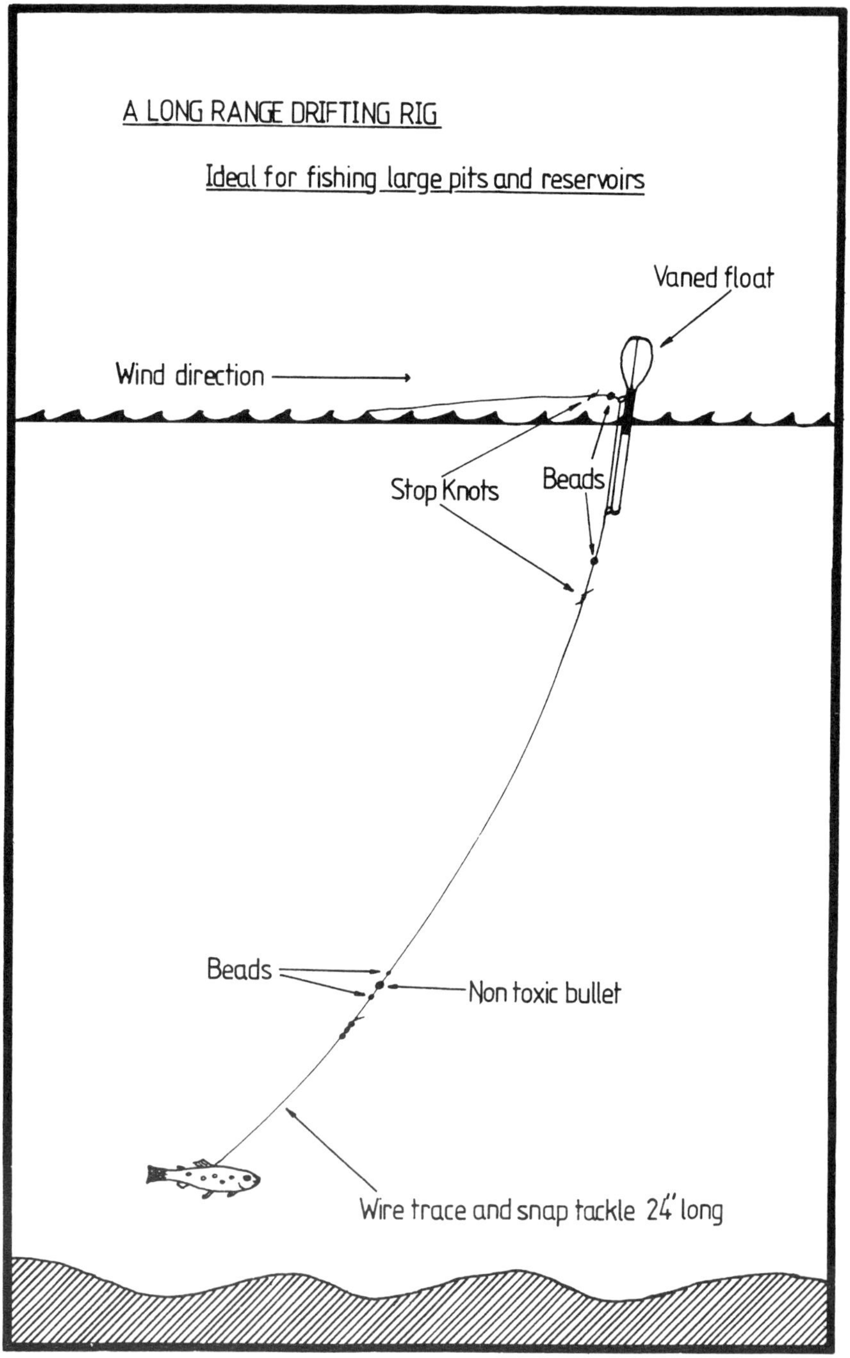
A LONG RANGE DRIFTING RIG
Ideal for fishing large pits and reservoirs
Vaned float
Wind direction
Stop Knots
Beads
Beads
Non toxic bullet
Wire trace and snap tackle 24" long

most of the other anglers on the water are using the same technique as each other.

A very simple example of when this may work is when the pike are fry-feeding, as they may well do in the area about a culvert mouth, or around a valve tower, for short spells each year. Most anglers will be float fishing a livebait close to the surface where the bulk of the fry are, and where the pike are visible. Between each strike, the pike are waiting in the deeper water, even close to the bottom. You may well find you do better by fishing a free-swimming float-fished livebait at least as deep as mid water, or paternostering a livebait within two feet of the bottom. I have emphasised a *live* bait because when fry feeding, pike do usually become preoccuppied with live fish, even on waters where at other times they are good deadbait feeders.

Long range drifting techniques often come into their own on reservoirs simply because holding areas, such as ridges, gulleys and plateaux, are just as likely to be found at 200 yards distance as any feature within casting range.

It doesn't always follow that on big waters the deeper areas are in the middle. Equally, depending entirely on the nature of the reservoir construction, or valley damming, the deepest water may be no more than 25 feet deep. Such depths are frequently visited by pike at all times of the year.

As daunting as some of the larger reservoirs may seem at first glance, their very size gives enormous scope for an individual approach. Equally as grim, at times, is the effect that weather has on the movements of the fish – not to say the angler! Strong-gusting winds are probably the worst condition the reservoir angler is likely to endure, and to be perfectly frank there is little virtue in sticking it out under such conditions. It may be possible to tuck away in some quiet area, though it is far more sensible to visit smaller fisheries less affected by the gale. As rough as it may become, the size and depth of many reservoirs render them amongst the last waters to freeze over during a cold spell, so there is one plus point. However, during very cold weather the results may become very slow indeed, for reasons which are not yet fully understood. It seems that many of the pike gather up, not necessarily into hotspots, but simply into groups which do not appear to feed at all regularly. Often these fish are a long way offshore, sometimes in deep water, but just as often in mid-water making fishing for them very difficult indeed. Keep in touch with the situation by all means, but fish with renewed enthusiasm when the weather breaks and those, by now hungry, pike come back on the feed.

The problems associated with the location of pike in the depths of winter are not isolated to reservoirs. Gravel pits, especially the open, large and deep ones, present exactly the same problems. Clearly, the key to sorting one out is connected with the depth of the fishery. I say this because by and large the pike in the shallow pits, especially those with lots of bars and islands, are easy enough to find at all times of the year.

It is necessary to generalise at times like this, although obviously there are exceptions to any case. As a general rule gravel-pit pike are wanderers. That is not to say that they are continuously on the move, because clearly such is not the case – hotspots are just as frequently located on gravel pits as on any other type of fishery. What does happen though is that the pike regularly, usually daily, follow the same beat, or patrol route, in search of food. Often these routes follow bars and islands and on each route there may be a resting-up spot, which may even be a genuine hotspot. Such holding areas are not necessarily areas of submerged trees, or weed or reed beds, although these are excellent and reliable places, year in and year out. The holding areas may be in open water without any obvious features. Sometimes it is possible to decide why a spot is favoured and look for similar features in other areas.

Some pits when excavated leave parallel rows of islands, usually running in the same direction, right across the pit. Every now and then there will be a break in this pattern, perhaps where a point sticks out from the bank or where the pit narrows. This usually leaves a bay, or a confluence of several channels, and these places are as good as anywhere to make a start. By fishing two baits, one in open water, the second close by an island (where the island's shelf drops quickly away into deeper water), you are fishing not only for patrolling fish, but also for any which may have rested up. Another area worthy of attention is a long island, especially if there are one or two 'breaks' in it allowing access to and from the channels to each side of it. The way to fish these places is to put two baits at different positions along the island. Cast one bait directly out in front and the other 20 or 30 yards down and across. If nothing happens either move along and repeat the process or bring one of the baits into open water, slowly working it back to your bank. Remember that your 'fishing' bank is effectively the margin of an island and your presence may deter pike from patrolling it. A third area to try along the same island is either right next to one of the gaps previously mentioned, or directly in the middle of it. Some patrolling pike will use this gap to switch to the next channel, rather than swim to the end of the island and then turn back.

Patrolling pike usually swim along their chosen routes at much the same depth, rather than erratically varying their position at 'whim'. Presumably they know from experience how best to approach any potential prey although there may well be other factors beyond the scope or this chapter affect or dictate this. In practical terms what this means is that you will have to determine this swimming depth by fishing; there is no easy answer. One way is to fish your baits (say) 2 feet off-bottom because, for starters, these will be seen by pike close to the bottom and

Large pike taken on half herring. (Photo: M. Gay)

probably from at least 4 feet off-bottom. If nothing happens but you know pike are in the area, simply vary the fishing depth.

Successful piking on gravel pits means fishing to some type of feature, and I would suggest that with the exception of the big deep-winter problem waters, finding a good feature is worth more in practice than looking for prey fish. (On reservoirs the reverse often prevails.) The two of course go hand in hand, because often an area patrolled by pike, or favoured as a resting place will be shared by the prey fish.

Other productive swims most certainly include my previously mentioned submerged trees, which were areas of growth before the excavation was flooded. Such swims are treacherous and should not be fished with anything other than heavy gear, and certainly at least 12 lb bs line. Almost needless to say the strike should be made the instant that the pick up is detected to prevent the pike from running into the trees. Bait positioning is difficult unless the trees are emergent, and fishing the fringes of these areas is not usually as productive as is fishing in gaps within the jungle. At all times the welfare of the fish must come first, so please use strong tackle to keep the pike high in the water, use small baits to facilitate a rapid strike and as few hooks on the bait as size will permit.

A large, open area of water at some distance from the bank is for some reason often a good spot. I couldn't call such areas hotspots but they are certainly holding areas, although potentially short lived. The pike may gather there because of the stability that a large area of water offers, or at times it may be that the fish find themselves almost herded into such areas because of their patrol routes along adjacent features.

Islands with heavy tree growth overhanging the water, especially if the trees shade a good depth of water, can be reliable because the cover affords protection and subdued light. I make quite a lot about finding a good depth of water – by which I mean 12 feet, down to 25 feet at times – because overall, large pike (fish upwards of say 10 lb) prefer such water. Perversely, the one time of the year when they actively seek out the shallows, sometimes the shallowest water, is at the time when the water may well be at its coldest. That is of course at the approach to spawning time.

Certainly in the southern half of the country pike will start to gather on the spawning grounds as early as December – the males preceding the females – although it may not be until late January or February that the largest concentrations are present. Then they will mill around until late March or early April before spawning. Pike on the spawning grounds are very catchable right up until the end of the season but the heavily spawn-laden females must be treated with the utmost care.

Minerals are extracted from some excavations in a terraced fashion. No bars or islands are present, the water merely getting deeper in steps. The most likely productive area will be on the edge of each step as the depth increases fairly rapidly, aiming again, at a depth of around 15 feet.

Young gravel pits in which the pike are fast growing, are likely to produce the best sport, although the potential for a very big fish will clearly not be there for several years. At this stage in the development of the fishery, the pike will probably take deadbaits and livebaits with equal enthusiasm. This may change as the angling pressure rises, and thereafter you may find a swing away from deadbaits, and an increase in the number of dropped runs. It pays to use sensitive bite detection methods, as small an amount of lead as you can get away with, and to vary the bait type to overcome the increasing wariness of the pike.

Strangely this above mentioned problem doesn't affect all pike on all waters, but it is as well to be aware of its potential. As the pit matures, the pike fishing is likely to level out with the sport being rather slow, but of course the potential size will increase for several years at least, probably to a ceiling weight of 25 to 28 lb. This situation can provide pike fishing at its very best, with good numbers of heavy-built double-figure pike, and some interesting problems to iron out.

As the years go by I become increasingly reluctant to advise on preferred weather conditions applicable to either reservoirs or gravel pits. In many cases both types of water are affected similarly, with sudden cold snaps usually putting the pike off feed until the temperatures stabilise at a new level. But even here there are enough exceptions to that generalisation to make me wary! A warm south-westerly at any time of the year is good, especially when it follows a prolonged cold spell, but you will find some waters which fish better in sunshine than others, irrespective of temperature and wind direction. A good policy, which should ultimately lead to consistent sport, is to concentrate on just two or three waters, if possible of different acreages and depths so that the vagaries of the weather can be worked around. Big, still waters go through dead spells, summer and winter, when nothing you do seems to work, and at such times it is sensible to have a small, shallow, pit or an old reservoir of modest size of retreat to. The pike, after all, are every bit as good!

Rainbow Trout Waters and their Record Breaking Potential

BILL WINSHIP

During the spring of 1984 I was criticised in the *Coarse Angler* magazine for suggesting that record-sized pike could still be found in several waters around the British Isles. Of course, at that time such a statement appeared over-optimistic because Hancock's 40 lb record had remained intact for almost twenty years.

However, within a few short months this controversial prophesy was fulfilled by the sudden appearance of several pike in excess of 40 lb in different parts of Britain. No less than five forties were taken by fisheries staff at Llandegfedd reservoir in Wales. Also taken were several other fish which came within ounces of the record, and of course the rod-caught record was finally broken by Amies/Fickling Pike in 1985.

New record pike have been predicted with confidence since the early seventies when game anglers introduced low-priced stock trout in mass quantities into our lowland still waters. This vast and unnatural influx of high-protein trout flesh was bound to improve growth rate and push existing weight ceilings to a new high. We now know that these factors have created new opportunities for the pike angler because they have enabled pike stocks all over Britain to grow to a very large average size indeed. Rainbow-fed pike are quite different in shape and appearance to the average stamp of fish. They are rounded in profile, deep in the flank and have very small heads in relation to their body, providing a characteristic young appearance.

Not surprisingly these fish enjoy a very fast growth rate, either two or three times that we are accustomed to on normal water. The following table compares these growth rates with some well-documented growth findings from Lomond pike.

There is always a temptation for the angler to look at rainbow trout waters like Lindholm Lake and project forward to the possible weight for a fifteen- or eighteen-year-old fish. Logically if such a water can produce a 30 lb fish in eight years then the upper limits for a fifteen-year-old fish could well exceed our current record fish, in theory.

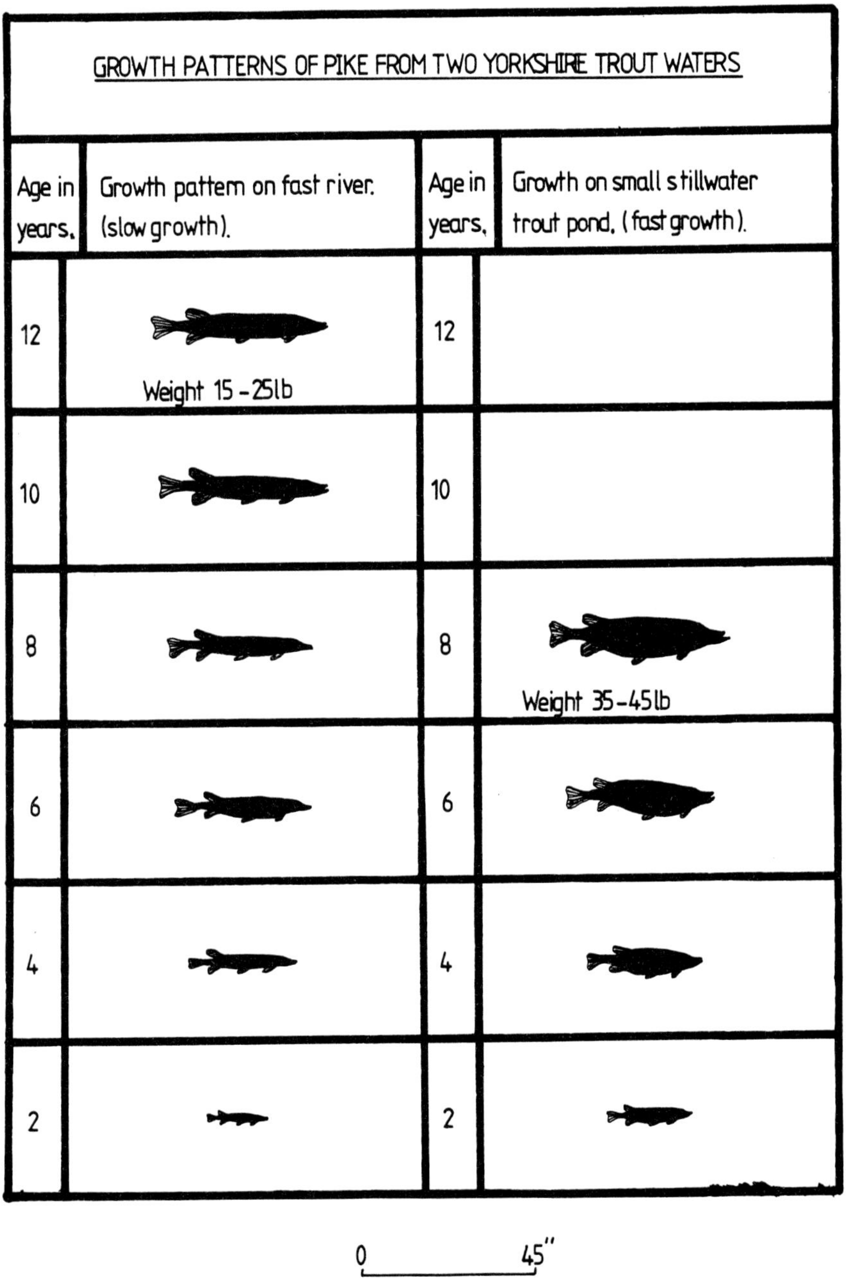
GROWTH PATTERNS OF PIKE FROM TWO YORKSHIRE TROUT WATERS
Age in years.
Growth pattern on fast river. (slow growth).
Age in years.
Growth on small stillwater trout pond. (fast growth).
12
Weight 15 - 25lb
12
10
10
8
8
Weight 35 - 45lb
6
6
4
4
2
2
0
45"

Pike growth rates of two well known waters:

Age (years)	Lindholm Lake Pike (lb) Rainbow trout plus wild coarse fish	Lock Lomond Pike (lb) Wild trout/salmon wild coarse fish
6	20	8
8	30	16
10	?	20
15	?	30

Unfortunately though, big thirties seem almost as rare in waters with fast growth as in those with slow growth rates. Furthermore no one seems to know for certain why there appears to be a universal shortage of older fish on fast growth waters. This has been outlined by Buller and Rickards in their literature on pike. However, there is a rational if somewhat complex explanation – but not too complex for the inquisitive angler.

The growth and life span of living organisms is largely predetermined genetically and the controlling information is stored in the cell nucleus. The specific age to which any animal can live is also limited to the number of times the living cell can copy itself. This copying process can be compared by analogy to the photocopying process where each reproduction of the previous copy becomes slightly impaired. This process of progressive deterioration is called ageing and continues until death occurs. The important point is that the actual number of copies possible is predetermined genetically within the living cell.

Buller has pointed out that growth is slow in relatively infertile surroundings like Windermere. Therefore in such a water cell reproduction, or copying, in pike is much reduced causing the fish to grow and age at a very gentle rate.

Compare the slow growth situation of Windermere pike to the fast growth and fast ageing process of pike in rainbow trout waters. It soon becomes obvious why a disproportionately low number of trout-water pike exceed the 32 lb barrier. In effect these rich-feed pike grow and age at such a fast rate that they become spent at a relatively young age. They grow so fast that they burn themselves out in a relatively short time. This 'burn out' theory may well explain why so few pike in excess of 32 lb are taken from the Great Western Fisheries of Ireland where the limestone-bedded loughs also promote fast growth rates. People like Fred Buller have pointed to a shortage of big pike on the Irish Loughs. Of course Fred Buller has also documented many pike in excess of 40 lb from the Irish Fisheries but these fish are obviously freak captures as

Trout fed pike. A brace of pike from Lindholm Lake (18 acres). Top fish 32 lb, bottom fish 20 lb, caught in the days when the lake was a trout fishery. (Photo: B. Winship)

A fat pike from a four acre rainbow trout water. Bill Winship has found that the small rainbow trout waters tend to produce the fattest pike. (Photo: B. Winship)

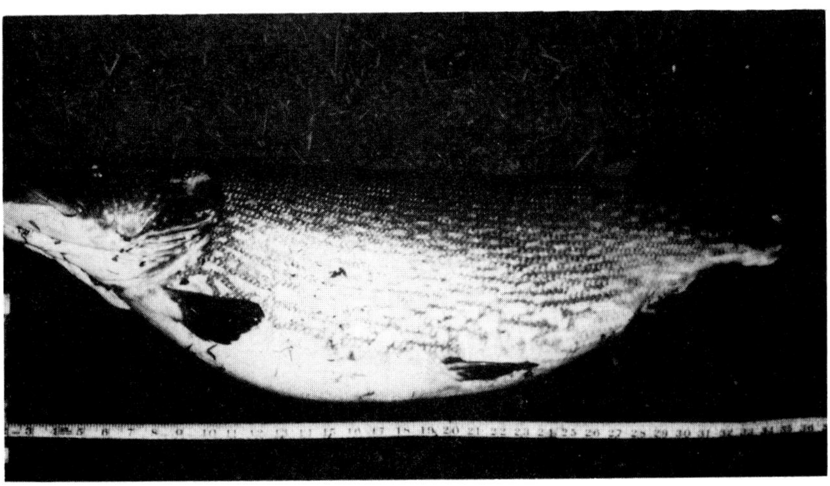

they only seem to occur intermittently over the decades.

Anyone who deliberately sets out to break a record should bear in mind that he is looking for freak fish, which are by definition very rare indeed. Such fish have been caught in all kinds of waters, including cold water environments like Windermere or Lomond. Only a few years ago Gordon Burton found a dead pike which he claims must have weighed more than 40 lb when it lived.

Although fast-growth waters are not the only ones capable of producing freak or record fish they do perhaps offer the best chance because they tend to produce a greater number of large fish each year.

Consequently the chances of catching such rarities are that much greater. Trout waters are arguably amongst the most likely to produce a new British record-pike in the forthcoming years.

The Pike: Age, Weight, Growth and Scale Interpretation

GEORGE SHARMAN

In previous centuries there was a common belief that some fish lived for many years . . . far beyond the normal human life-span. Carp, for instance, were thought to live for between 100 and 150 years, whilst pike were thought to have lived for over 200 years. These were not old wives tales; they were stories that were actually published in works on natural history in the eighteenth and nineteenth centuries.

AGE

In more recent times Dr Regan thought that the carp might live for up to fifty years under artificial conditions. In the wild he was doubtful if the carp would exceed fifteen years. Chapman Pincher thought that mirror carp live for forty-seven years. My experience suggests that carp will live for between forty and fifty years, with wild carp exceeding that. Dr Regan also thought that pike of 60 to 70 lb in weight might well be at least as many years old. Chapman Pincher says that pike live for only fourteen years. My experience here is that I have read many scales from large pike that have grown for longer than fourteen years, the oldest so far being seventeen years of growth. I feel fairly confident in stating that carp *grow* for up to fifteen years, and pike *grow* for up to eighteen years. The major problem facing anybody who looks for scientific proof of age in these long-lived fish, is that when the fish stops growing there is no further record left to mark the passing years. My own views on this matter are simply that most of the evidence from the animal kingdom generally shows that the longer it takes an animal to become fully grown, the longer is its total life-span.

There is the story of the 'Emperor's Pike' that was first quoted by Gesner in 1558. This enormous pike was taken in a lake near Württemburg in 1497. A copper ring was found encircling the gill region. There was an inscription on the ring that said the pike had been placed in the lake by Emperor Frederick the Second, in the year 1230 –

some 267 years prior to the pike being caught! The pike was said to be 19 feet long and to weigh 550 lb. The skeleton of this monster pike was reputed to be in the cathedral at Mannheim. Sometime during the last century it was studied by a German anatomist, who found that there were too many vertebrae in the backbone for the skeleton to belong to a single individual . . . it would appear that somebody had been at work lengthening the skeleton to fit the tale.

It occurred to me that you might like to know if the length fitted the weight in this old legend. Well, really, we are in the age when dragons weighing several tons flew and, if that isn't enough, they were also supposed to blow flames from their nostrils! However, calculations show that a 19 foot pike ought to weigh at least 3,000 lb in decent condition. Conversely, if we take the weight quoted, of 50 lb, the pike would have been about 10½ feet long. these figures are based on the normal constants obtained from normal pike. The 'Emperor's Pike' was anything but normal and would have looked something like a aquatic flag pole!

There is no doubt, though, that most species of fish grow to a superior size on the Continent. In England we have to accept that smaller specimens are likely. Scotland and Ireland have both produced some very big pike from their lochs and loughs. In theory there is no reason why this state of affairs should exist, though it is generally accepted that large waters produce large pike. Given that pike require a regular and wide ranging food supply to satisfy their growth needs, it might be expected that a well stocked lake would provide a better environment than a deep, cold, acidic Scottish loch. So why don't we regularly catch 50 lb pike from our English waters? Well, the only logical answer I can see is that there is too much angling pressure and many pike don't live long enough to reach their full potential.

A realistic look at the average pike water will show that not many anglers are needed to fish the water to saturation level using modern methods. It would need an army and considerable time to do the same in a loch. There are basic laws at work here and, in the average water, the first law is that the angler will have a good chance of showing all the pike, large and small, the bait he is fishing. The second law is that any water can only supply and support a limited number of large predators during a given time period: becoming large in an environment takes time, so the chance of being caught increases as the fish grows larger. It is when the pike is in big doubles or early twenties that the third law, that of gravity, begins to make the right handling very important. Large fish of any species need careful treatment to avoid damage on the bank. Large pike, in particular, would seem more vulnerable to gill, stomach and, possibly, swim-bladder damage while being handled. After about twenty years of involvement with specimen fish and specimen groups,

I know that no specialist angler would cause undue harm to a large fish. Nevertheless, I still think it is worth pointing out some of the less appreciated dangers.

We have seen earlier that there is evidence to show that pike ought to be able to live for a long time. To make sure large specimens have every chance we must be prepared to use a little imagination when we have one on the bank. One of the things I remember about the first decent pike I saw, was that its gills looked very exposed and easily damaged. Apart from the physical damage that can occur, there is a more insidious one that may be overlooked. The wide gill-raker spacing of the predatory pike has, unlike most cyprinid fish, very little ability to retain water to keep the gill filaments moist. If the fish is out of the water for a long time there is a danger that the gills will dry out and the fish will suffocate. With most fish, the heart and liver are close to the pectoral fins – just the place most guys hold a pike when posing for a mug shot; how many shots have you seen where the hand is sinking deep at this point? Big pike are more flaccid than other large fish, no doubt because of their large stomach. But fingers sink into the belly when lifting and result in high pressure being applied in relatively small areas of the stomach. Consider, then, that the pike may have eaten a few perch before being caught. Perch have spines and sharp operculae that would digest slower than the softer flesh, as would the sharp, needle-like, bones of other fish. Any external pressure on the belly above a critical level may force some of these bones through the stomach wall. This could well cause a leakage of acid and food particles into the body cavity and would eventually cause death from peritonitis.

The swim bladder is normally situated between the stomach and the backbone, running from the front to rear. Any bones penetrating the stomach may also rupture the swim bladder. You will appreciate that while a small hole in the relatively thick stomach wall might heal, the thin, balloon-like, swim-bladder would not be able to inflate. This hydrostatic organ is inflated with a high percentage of nitrogen in our freshwater fish. It occupies about 8.5 per cent of the body volume and allows the fish to vary its hydrostatic equilibrium, so that it can rise, fall or hold still in mid-water without using any energy other than that required to alter the amount of gas in the bladder. Anyone who has studied the pike in the water – seeing how it stalks its prey, moving so very gently, lining up and slowly winding up the powerful body muscles until the body becomes S shaped just before the lightening strike is made – will know how very important the precise control given by the swim bladder is to the pike's survival. While the pike could still swim along without a swim-bladder, it would sink to the bottom as soon as it stopped. It might live off the bottom for a while, or catch a few fish by actively chasing after them, but it would not be able to ambush fish, using little energy in the process, and would eventually die of starvation.

Gut-hooked pike are not the problem they used to be in the past because pike anglers have improved their techniques tremendously over the last decade. I know it is possible to remove hooks from deep inside but it does make me wonder what damage is caused to the stomach wall. The angler isn't always to blame for a gut-hooked pike; sometimes it happens because the pike just gulps down the bait. Whether this is intended or accidental, I don't know. I remember pike fishing with a friend many years ago. American plugs were the 'in' things for pike fishing at the time, mainly due to the influence of two successful pike anglers called Fred Wagstaff and Bob Reynolds. (They both presented papers on the subject at the Third British Angling Conference in 1972.) My companion was using one of these plugs: a large jointed floater, the name of which escapes me at the time of writing. He cast the plug under the far bank close to a bush and the moment it landed, it disappeared in a tremendous upheaval of water. Without time for a strike, the rod slammed over and my friend found himself playing a double. The fish did not fight well and when it was landed we found that it had almost completely swallowed the plug. We managed to get the plug out, in spite of those enormous hooks, but I would not give a deal for its chance of surviving the ordeal.

In any summary of pike longevity we must be aware of, and make allowance for, a reduction in life-span that might be caused by accidental damage when hooking, handling and unhooking. Generally speaking the major problem in the sequence will be handling. Big fish are virtually weightless in water; they live in an 'inner space' environment, where pressure is evenly distributed over the entire body. In the generally shallow freshwater environment the increase in pressure is not very high and the fish is designed to cope with 'all over pressure' at a fair depth. On land the full effect of gravity comes into play and small areas support all weight of the fish's body. The safe way to move pike on the bank is to carry them in the net and avoid lifting by hand as much as possible. Transfer from landing net to weigh net is best done by rolling the pike from one side, onto its back, then onto the other side. If the weigh net is correctly placed it will receive the fish without any lifting and without any excessive pressure being placed on the stomach or other vulnerable parts.

To conclude this section on age we ought to give some thought to what happens when a large fish is injured. Like most wild animals it will seek a secure place to hide until it recovers. This might be a reed or weed bed or even an undercut bank. Should the fish die, the safe place becomes a possible trap which may hold the body and keep it from being seen. Eventually, when the body disintegrates, the bones will sink into the mud and leave no trace of its former existence. Some pike do float to the surface when they die and it is a worrying fact that reported findings of dead pike are quite common . . . and the pike are usually big. When this happens there is often some controversy about the original weight. Many pike found like this are under average weight for length, which suggests that they have taken some time to die and not eaten in the period. There is talk, often confused, about the body being 'water logged' and it might be an idea to look at the process of osmosis to see what is involved.

The blood and body tissue of freshwater fish contains more salt than the surrounding water. There is an effect called osmosis which occurs across permeable membranes like gills and skin. Because fluids can pass through such membranes, there is a tendency for the body salts to leak out and the water to soak in, thus diluting the blood and tissue. When the fish is alive it can overcome this dilution by producing more salts from the food it eats and by urinating large quantities of weak urine that is almost entirely water. When the fish dies the heavier salts leak away and allow the less dense water to leak into the body tissues. This should make the fish *lighter* than when it was alive. However, if the large stomach is empty and that fills with water, it will provide additional weight to offset that lost from the body tissue. In the end much may depend upon how much weight has been lost below the average for the length of the particular fish, as to whether the dead weight is representative or not.

WEIGHT

Weight and growth are, for the greater part of the pike's life, synonymous. Any increase in one will be matched directly by an increase in the other. There are a few circumstances in which this general rule does not apply: when the pike is carrying spawn, when the pike has just finished spawning, and when it has finished growing. These points will be discussed in more detail later.

When calculations using weight and length are made, it is possible to find a condition factor for a fish. This condition factor is important because it reduces the weight and length to a number that can then be compared easily with a similar number obtained from other pike. Pike grow in an *allometric* way, which means that as a fish grows it becomes heavier per inch: a ten-inch pike would weigh 0.5 oz per inch; a twenty-inch pike would weigh 2 oz per inch. This becomes even more pronounced as the pike grows larger. A table of pike weights and lengths was first published in the *Fishing Gazette* in 1918. It was supplied by a contributor who wrote under the name of Mona and the list became known as Mona's Scale. Since that time the same formula has been used and has appeared variously as Fulton's Coefficient of Condition, in graph form from Merriman (1941) and in work by Beckman (1948), to name just a few who have used the expression. It can be employed to compare pike from different waters, to find seasonal variations in the same water, or to plot weight/length distribution as the fish grows.

Mona's Scale uses a cube law formula that provides a table showing that as a fish grows and *doubles* its length, it will weigh *eight times* more. It is shown like this: W/L^3, where W is the weight of the fish, L is the length, and 3 is the cubing factor. The product of the expression is a number called K, or the constant. As an introduction to the use of constants and how the information they produce is used, the following may be of interest. About ten years ago I went through all the pike weights and lengths I had collected from various sources. There were several hundred and I hasten to add that I did not catch the fish, I was just interested in weight and growth and used the material to feed my interest. After working out the condition factor of every fish, the total was divided by the number of fish used, to produce a common factor for pike. The common factor was 0.0052 and if the cubed length of a pike is multiplied by this number it will give the average weight of the fish at that length. The full decimal fraction must be used in any calculations, but I reduced the figure to simply 52 for easier use in correspondence comparisons. Using the same information produced by the work, I was able to select and set the lower and upper condition factors. I can tell you that a *low* condition is 40 (0.0040) and a *high* condition is 65 (0.0065). These are not the maximum extremes but they are not often exceeded. Using a calculator to work-out and compare your pike catches is very simple indeed, and can provide an interesting close season exercise. It is important to remember that all my figures and constants are based on *ounces* and *inches*. Lets have a look at growth now, and use condition factors to see how a pike's weight alters as it grows.

GROWTH

A pike begins life as an egg of 2.5 to 3.0 mm in diameter (Pincher 1947). The time it will take for a pike egg to hatch depends on water temperature: it will take five days at 15 degrees centigrade, and twenty-five days at 5 degrees centigrade (Lindroth 1946); Lillelund (1967) gives nine days at 12.2 degrees centigrade. The eggs are ripe and ready for spawning to commence any time from February to May (Pincher). The number of eggs produced is directly related to the size of the fish and has been proved by many workers, three of the earliest being Raitt (1933), Pincher (1947) and Le Cren (1951). I have not been able to find a reference to the weight of a single egg. My calculations suggest a weight of one ten thousandth of an ounce might be an acceptable figure. I feel it is important to know the weight of a single egg, because if we know how many eggs the pike carries at spawning time, we can calculate how much more it will weigh.

When the egg hatches, the tiny pike is only a fraction of an inch long. It hangs vertically from aquatic plants for two or three weeks until development is complete. Then it will start hunting small creatures like water fleas and other immature aquatic animals before taking fish. I think it was Dr Frost (I have lost the reference) who said that pike in Windermere lived on the larvae of caddis flies and dragon-flies and crustacea until they were two or more years old. My own observation of pike suggests this is not the case in every water. In the river Witham in the mid-sixties I witnessed several tiny pike, approximately one inch long, ambushing and eating even smaller cyprinid fish as the shoal swam past their hiding place. No doubt they take advantage of the most suitable food supply that is available.

Pike grow very well during the first few years. Their condition factors are quite low, being about 45 at 18 inches, up to 49 at 25 inches. Throughout this early period pike are long and thin. Soon after this the growth curve becomes steeper, and at a body length of 27 inches the condition factor is 52. This condition phase is held until the pike reaches something like 33 inches. After that, for the next five or six inches of growth, the curve increases still more to give a condition factor of 54. From the information I have collected many pike seem to be in their best condition when they are above 40 inches long. Between 39 and 41 inches the condition factor is around 55 and the average 41 inch pike will weigh about 24 lb. From 45 inches upwards there seems to be a gradual decline in body condition, from 57 at 45 inches down to 44 at 55 inches, where I would expect the average pike to weigh 45 lb 12 oz. All of the foregoing is the result of my own work on weight and growth. All the figures quoted are based on the average weight of many pike at a given length. There are bound to be differences in the norm at different venues, but the intention is that a reliable average range of weight/length will allow comparison.

I have prepared two graphs that illustrate the average growth curve. One is my own which has been plotted using 215 pike weighing between 12 oz and 51 lb 9 oz. (I had to rely on continental pike for the upper register of this graph. However, their condition factors are no different to ours on the whole – they just grow bigger – so I am quite satisfied that the figures quoted are reliable.) The other graph has been plotted using the weights and lengths obtained from Mona's Scale. Mona used one 40 inch pike weighing 20 lb to formulate his scale; generally it isn't too bad as an average, but tends to be heavy at top and bottom and light in the middle.

We have seen that as pike grow there is an exponential increase in weight. When pike are old enough to spawn there is a significant increase in weight with virtually no growth to accompany it. The vast

PIKE WEIGHT FOR LENGTH GRAPH
215 pike
12 oz to 51 lb 9 oz

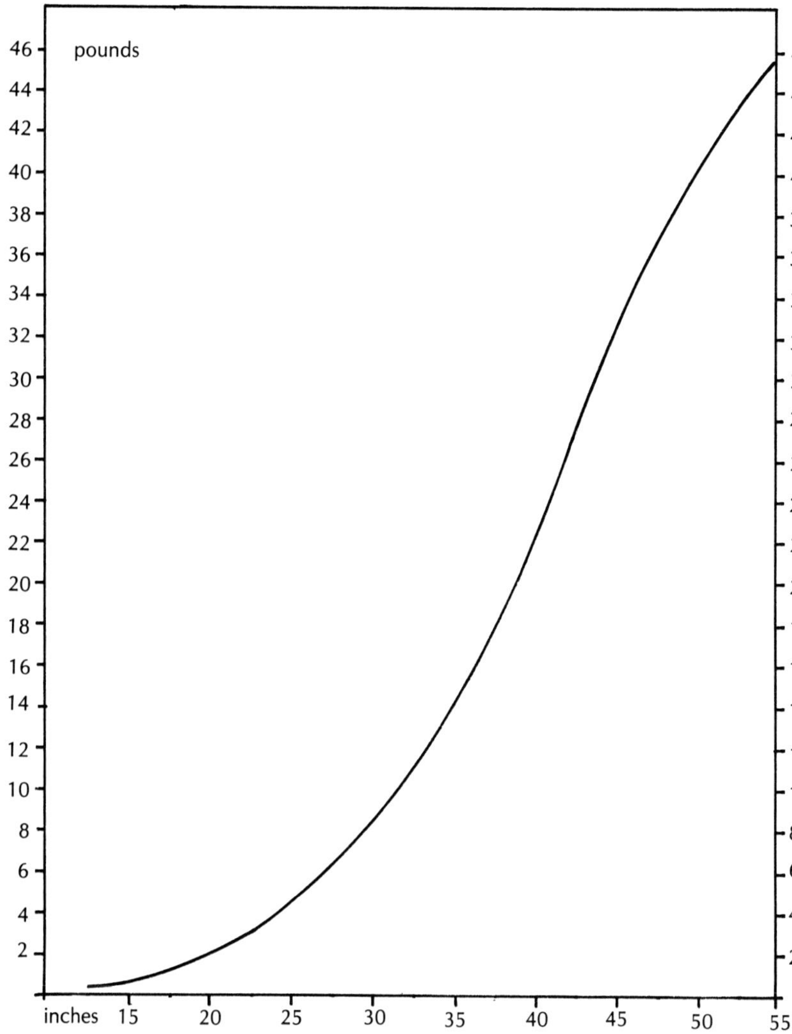

MONA'S PIKE SCALE CONVERTED TO GRAPH FORM

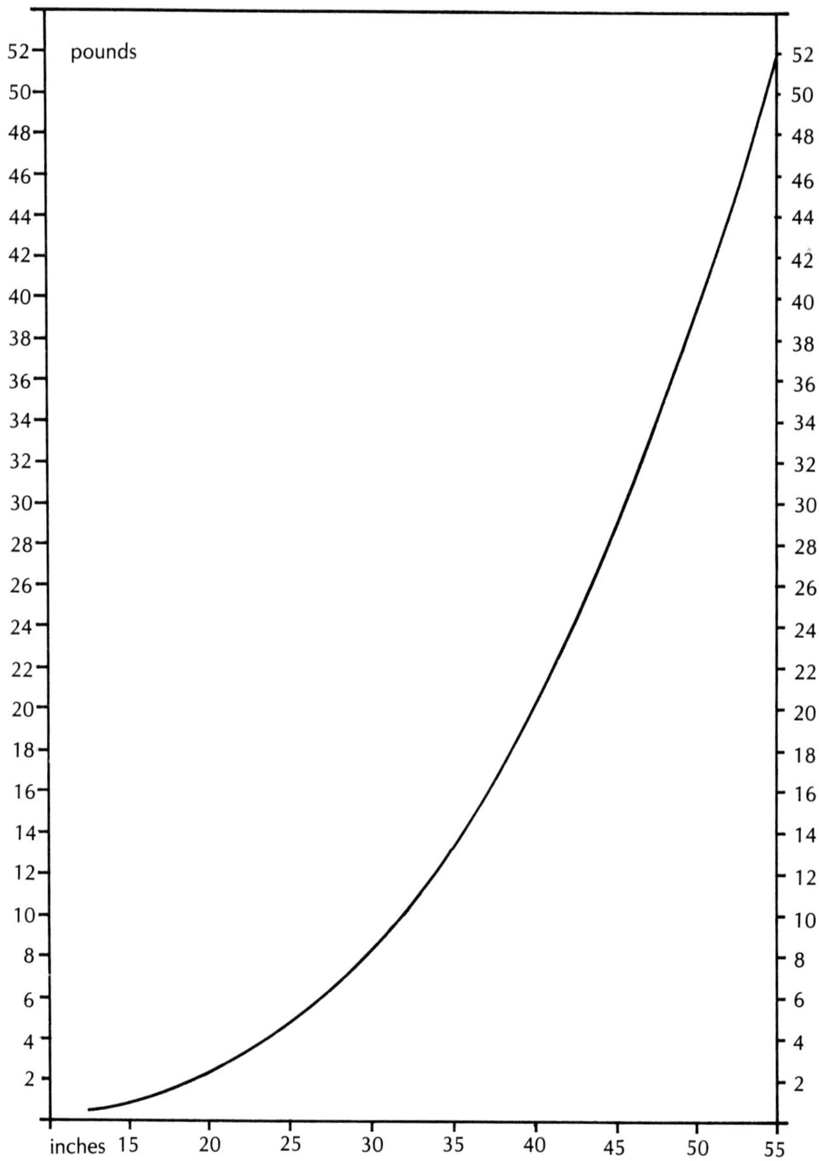

number of eggs being carried make the fish fatter than normal and increase the condition factor by ten or more prior to spawning. That means a pike that has a factor of 55 most of the year will have one of 65 at spawning time. It will also be about an inch longer without having grown, this being due entirely to it being rounder. Scale reading reveals that serious spawning commences when the fish is about six years old. Male pike may well be able to produce viable sperm before they are six years old, but the female is faced with a far greater task in terms of egg weight / body weight. I think she will be older than the male before being fully viable at spawning time. Certainly pike scales do not show serious absorption until they are six or seven years old. I have always thought that the reabsorbed areas in scales are laid down during and just after spawning, when the fish is recovering from the effort of a prolonged spell of activity, little feeding, and the loss of between ten and twenty per cent of body weight. Another factor supporting this view is that the growth rate drops dramatically when reabsorbed areas are evident. In my view this is because something like half the amount of food the pike eats in a year is used for, and disappears in, the process of procreation. All fish lose weight at spawning time and I often wonder if the record fish are just exceptional growers, or if they are sterile or not given to spawning at the same intensity as average females. There ought to be a market for sterilised females to stock good pike waters.

Pike produce good numbers of eggs at their peak when the ovaries are fully ripe. Pincher (1947) gives the following number of ripe eggs from actual egg counts that were done on female pike of the weights listed:

Weight *lb oz*	*Number of* *ripe eggs*
6 – 08	136,000
10 – 00	149,000
23 – 00	224,000
32 – 00	595,000

So if a single egg weighs about one ten thousandth of an ounce, as proposed earlier, the thirty-two above would be carrying about 3 lb 12 oz of eggs just prior to spawning. Apart from the egg weight pike are in excellent condition during the last month of the season and, while most fish are difficult to catch as spawning time approaches, there is reward for the successful angler. A pike of 26 lb can well be 31–32 lb in the last month of the season.

When the pike is fully grown the annual weight will fluctuate with the food supply in a purely natural environment. The condition factor will be high in the years when the cyprinids spawn well and low when severe weather causes heavy mortality on the spawning beds. There may, of course, be some overlap here, in that several good years might be followed by one or more bad ones. There will be a time, too, towards the later years of the pike's life-span, when it no longer takes part in the wasteful spawning routine. This will be the time when the condition factor is likely to reach the highest peak in the pike's life, though it might not keep this condition for more than a season or two.

FISH SCALE INTERPRETATION

A fish scale is made of bone similar to our finger nails and is constructed with grooves to allow it to flex as the fish swims along. The scale contains the whole story of growth, food supply, hard times and reproduction in a complex message of ridges and bands that run around it. Trying to read the message with accuracy is very difficult and is really a matter of trying to balance known facts with experienced guesswork, rather than a science. As scales grow, ridges are produced which are called radial striae. A good scale will have these growth ridges in evidence right from the centre to the edge. Sometimes a scale is lost when the fish is caught and, though it will grow back into place in a few weeks, the new scale will not be of any use in scale reading work. This type is called a replacement or cast scale. Such a scale is easily identified because it has an opaque look to it and no growth ridges or light and dark bands. Generally speaking, the best way to avoid cast scales is to take them from the shoulder area of the fish. On the whole I have not found scales 'picked out of the net' very reliable. The majority are from along the lateral line, which are poor for reading, and invariably have been cast before due to massive acceleration forces in this area, or have been lost during struggles in the net. The other major objection I have to scales found in the net is that one or more of those found may have been overlooked from a previous fish, thus confusing the person trying to sort out the growth message. The right way is to take the scales from the fish, put them in a plastic envelope and mark date, weight, and length clearly on the outside, or on paper placed inside. This simple information is of enormous help to anybody who eventually looks at the scales. It is normal to supply at least two sample scales, one from each shoulder. Four is a better sample because it allows more scope for growth comparison between scales, and allows any false checks to be evaluated.

False checks can cause some difficulty because they look similar to the normal annual checks that are read to age the fish. They can be identified, as a rule, by looking to see if they go right round the scale, as they are frequently incomplete. The true annual check can be traced all the way round the scale. The Loch Lomond scale photograph shows a faint false check between the second and third years. (I had to over-expose this print to bring out the false check from the other growth.) False checks only occur occasionally and are not always present on all the scales taken from a particular fish. There is still some doubt about the way false checks are laid down. Some think they are caused by a partial check in growth due to some environmental problem. I cannot accept this view because false checks only appear on some scales, as previously mentioned. In the late sixties I proposed in correspondence with Dr Cragg-Hine that false checks might be caused by scale disturbance when a fish is handled, leading to a disruption in growth and leaving a partial check. He accepted that it was a reasonable explanation and mentioned it in a later paper on scale reading. Fortunately, false checks seem more likely to appear on cyprinids, only rarely being seen on pike scales.

One of the things you have to watch out for at certain times is closely spaced checks. Normally, close checks occur towards the end of the growing period, but they can be seen on some individuals in other circumstances: when they start to spawn, when the fish has been ill, or when it has been injured in some way. The result is less growth than that normally shown in contemporaries from the same water in the same year. The causes can be many and varied but the end product is close checks that could be read as one, making the fish appear younger than it is. I have often noticed a distance of less than 1 mm between checks in pike scales, even though they have been enlarged ten or twelve times to reveal such detail.

Most fish grow well prior to becoming sexually mature. My experience with scale reading suggests that big fish, like pike and carp, don't begin to produce eggs until they are around five years old. My reason for thinking this is based upon the annual checks seen in the scales prior to five or six years of age; they usually appear as incomplete and oddly-spaced striae. After this time, when the fish can produce viable eggs, the annual check becomes an area of reabsorbed scale material that looks translucent when it is compared with the more opaque growth on either side of it. These areas of reabsorbed material are said to be caused when the fish requires certain elements more quickly than they can be supplied by other means at a time of need. This time of need can occur in times of food shortage, but the most common time is at and just after spawning when extra calcium is needed. This is taken from the scales in the form of calcium salts and leaves behind the previously mentioned reabsorbed areas. In the late sixties I was working on roach scales as part of a Hallamshire Group project. Looking at the two dimensional microscopic view suggested, the areas of reabsorbed material were like deep clefts in the normal growth. I prepared, mounted and polished some cross-sections and a friend and fellow member was able to photomicrograph the sectioned samples at four hundred and one thousand

A scale from a 28 lb Loch Lomond pike. (Photo: G. Sharman)

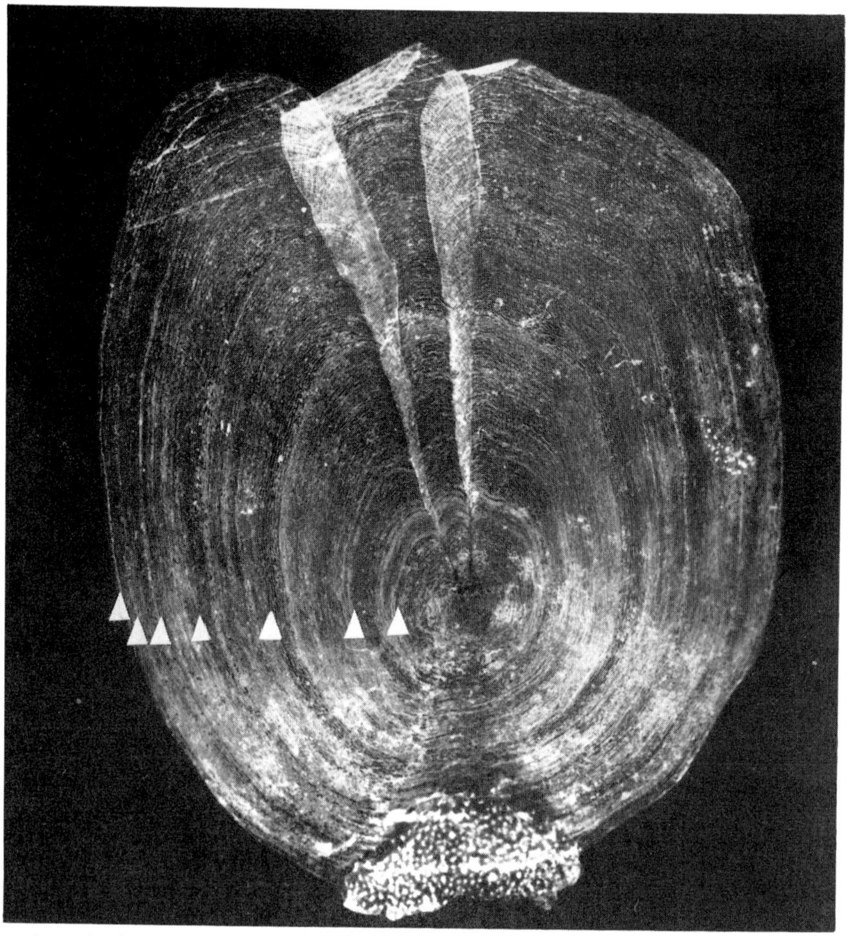

A scale from a relief channel pike. (Photo: G. Sharman)

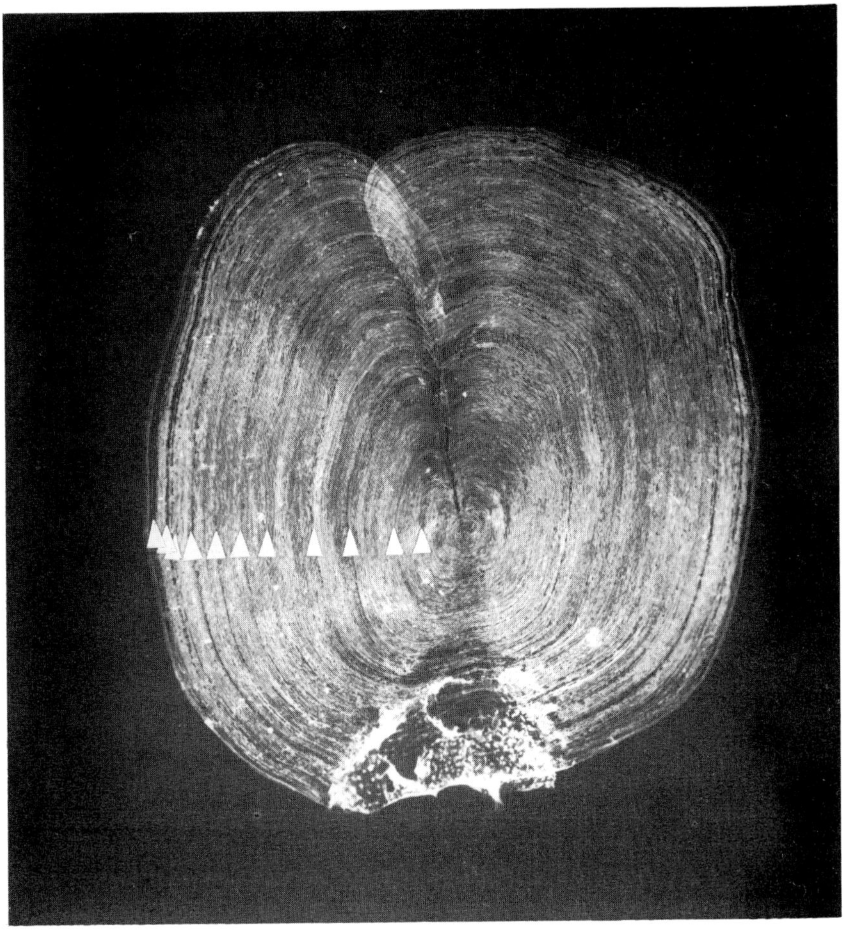

A scale from a 10 lb pike. (Photo: G. Sharman)

times magnification. These photographs revealed that the areas of reabsorption were, indeed, massive areas of collapse, where the original scale material appeared to have been 'sucked' inwards. Although these were photographs of roach scales I think the results are applicable to other species too. One final point here concerns the use of the word 'reabsorbed' to describe the material taken from the scales. As this material is taken in for use elsewhere a better word might be *absorption* as this infers that the material is incorporated into something else.

It is fortunate that spawning follows the winter period. The winter check and spawning check become incorporated and integrated into one. This provides a much clearer indication for the would be scale reader than was available before spawning commenced. When absorption is taking place the fish is losing weight, and it is generally accepted that it is 'living off its own body' during this time. Condition factors do show that many carp and pike are in rather poor condition, with low weight for length, for long periods after spawning. This reduced condition is caused by the comparatively sudden loss of thousands of eggs and the fishes' drop in body weight. The overall effects of spawning seem to be traumatic enough to leave severe marks on the scales.

As the fish grows older, the last few annual checks made before growth actually stops are liable to be closely spaced. Another product of this movement towards maximum growth is that the scale also becomes thicker as it grows larger. Less light is able to pass through the central regions of the scale and this can sometimes make the earlier years of growth difficult to pinpoint. This is another place to exercise care when trying to establish how many years the fish has grown. The first two years can often be quite hard to place and the experience gained from looking at scales taken from young fish is invaluable here. While most individual pike grow at different rates, there is a norm that can be established in most cases by looking at scales from fish only two or three years old. At the other end of the growth spectrum, when the fish has been fully grown for a number of years, or if it has been going through a bad environmental period, there is sometimes severe reabsorption right at the edge of the scale. The photograph of the ten pound pike shows this feature and there is the possibility that two previous checks have been obliterated by the material having been taken from the scale. As you will appreciate, if the first check is missed and two are reabsorbed from the outer edge, the fish would appear to have grown better than it has.

There isn't a great deal more I can say on scale reading. It is very difficult to teach anybody to read scales by using the written word. I have told you some of the things that you must look out for, and what sort of scales are best for interpretation, but it really is something you have to take part in to learn. I know full well that many anglers are only interested in the actual fishing and could not care less about work of this nature. But I also know that there are others who are prepared to put time and effort into this type of study and its is for them that I accepted the offer of submitting a chapter of this nature. So remember, start with young fish of any species, the younger the better, providing there is at least one check present! Do not be tempted to use aquarium fish or garden-pond fish because they may not show clear annual checks. I remember taking two scales from our pet goldfish to look at when I first started scale reading. We had kept the fish for about five years and it had increased its original length several times (it was all the maggots and worms I fed it on!). I was most disappointed to find that there were no checks on the scale at all. The exercise did show, though, that if fish suffer no winters or summers, or spawning or food shortage, then no checks appear on their scales, just steady growth all the way.

The future of pike fishing looks very good. We have seen the record change hands and several forty pounders caught in the last few seasons. Fifty pounds seems less remote than once thought. There has been a lot of interest in the exceptional pike caught from trout waters with the assumption that trout are better food and make pike grow bigger. After looking at the basic facts I don't think that pike do grow any better on trout than they do on other species. A well-stocked trout water may well supply the pike with an easier meal than the average coarse fishery. While trout do feed on the bottom, a lot of their time is spent cruising around mid-water or near the surface, looking for nymphs rising or stuck in the surface film. The pike is designed to attack from below the intended victim. It has upward-looking binocular vision that can lock onto a slowly cruising trout far more easily than onto a flashing shoal of roach. I think this is the basic reason why pike may grow bigger in trout waters; they have less trouble catching a decent meal.

Small pike do have difficulty in obtaining their daily food supply. I have watched them stalking roach many times in the margins and it is amazing how, after spending an age lining up on the victim, the strike fails. The roach always seem to be aware of what the pike is trying to do and, although the strike is lethally fast, most times the roach just lifts slightly in the water, allowing the pike to flash by harmlessly underneath. Big pike have the advantage of a much larger mouth, giving a greater cavitation effect. Before the strike is made the pike extrudes all the water from the mouth, which causes a flattening of the head. Then, a fraction of a second before the strike is made, a large cavity is formed within the closed mouth by muscular action. As the pike surges forward the mouth opens and the flood of water rushing into the mouth to fill the large vacuum carries the prey with it, overwhelming any attempt at escape. A big pike only has to get near to the victim and time the opening of the mouth correctly to make successful strikes on most occasions. The ability to obtain more food with less effort is reflected in the improved condition factor when the pike exceeds 27 inches in length.

The explanation given of why pike grow big in trout waters may have left a question mark in many people's minds. Perhaps they have been programmed to accept that trout have a higher protein level than other fish and are more suitable to promote extra growth. It is one of those plausible explanations that are sometimes trotted out without being given deeper thought. In fact there is no significant difference in the protein levels of most freshwater fish. In *A History of Fishes*, by J. R. Norman, the following is quoted:

Name	*Water*	*Protein*	*Fats*	*Calories (per lb)*
Carp	78.9	15.79	4.77	495
Bream	78.7	16.19	4.09	473
Pike	79.5	18.76	0.66	377
Perch	78.8	18.45	1.40	402
Trout	80.5	17.96	0.74	365

In theory the list shows that pike ought to be the best food for pike. A predator relying on rapid acceleration needs good muscle development, and a high protein, low fat diet ought to provide this best. Big females are said to eat quite a number of the smaller males, particularly at spawning time. I have not witnessed this personally, but it would make good economical sense. It is significant, anyway, that pike have the most protein and the least fat of the fish listed. Of course, if the pike angler wants slow, heavy pike, the best food on the list would seem to be carp or bream!

In conclusion to this chapter, let me say that I am extremely grateful for the opportunity to express my long-held, but unpublished, views on the pike. Age and growth interpretation has provided me with much interest during the last twenty years. Apart from the straightforward age and growth information, the interest has given me an insight into the life of fish – an insight that might only be possible by close study of the environmental effects left on the fishes' scales. It is my hope that this small contribution will generate sufficient interest in others to continue the study and to provide accurate information for future generations of pike anglers.

BIBLIOGRAPHY

During the preparation of this chapter reference was made to the following books and papers.

Clegg, J., *Pond Life*, 1956

Cragg-Hine, D., *Age Determination in Coarse Fish*, 1966

Cragg-Hine, D., *Scale Reading* (2 nd British Angling Conference), 1970

Hickling, C. F., *Fish Culture*, 1971

Jacques, D., *The Development of Modern Stillwater Fishing*, 1974

Norman, J. R., *A History of Fishes*, 1962

Greenwood, P. H.

Ottaway, E. M., *Growth Rates of fish and Their Use*, 1976

Simkiss, K.

Pincher, C., *University Library, Leeds*, 1947

Ricker, W. H., *Methods for Assessment of Fish Production in Freshwater*, —1971

Rounsefell, G. A., *Fishery Science. Its Methods and Applications*, 1953

Everhart, W. H.

Willock, C., *The Anglers' Encyclopaedia*, 1960

Weather, Season and the Feeding Behaviour of Pike

BILL WINSHIP

Fishermen have always recognised that there are certain links between weather conditions and the feeding behaviour of fish. They have also been very much aware that sporting prospects can be improved by understanding the relationship. Yet the task of pinpointing the essential ingredients of 'good' weather has always been a stumbling block and it is such a vast subject that it is difficult to know how to start in trying to make sense of it all.

One good way is to start by recording meteorological variables like air and water temperatures, sunlight and rainfall, and then check angling results against the collected records. If this is carried out carefully and over a long period of time the results can provide some useful and positive conclusions. My own studies of this subject are unusual in the sense that they have been compiled over many years, and are based on observations taken throughout the whole calendar year. These observations include details of water and air temperature, wind strength, sunshine and any other notable conditions thought to be relevant on the day.

Whenever this information is used to isolate the 'best' conditions for catching pike I always find it difficult to compare different seasons. I have found that favourable conditions in August can often be disastrous in November and vice versa. Yet when I concentrate on like months – say eight successful August periods – I have found that the weather conditions which bring success are repeated again and again. This is very encouraging because it suggests that the effects of weather on feeding behaviour are not simply a matter of chance, but rather happen for very good reasons, and for reasons which can be anticipated. These observations have led me to the conclusion that the best way to consider the effects of weather on feeding behaviour is to do so within the context of clearly stated months of the year. For this reason I have structured this section on a month by month basis starting with June.

Before doing this however, it is important to understand a few basic things about the biology of pike and, in particular, the way they react to changing water conditions. Without this information it is impossible to understand why pike change their feeding habits at different times of the year.

Firstly, it is important to understand that, as the pike is a cold-blooded, or poikilothermic, creature, its body temperature is the same as, or only a few degrees above, its surroundings. This makes the pike dependent upon temperature change: its bodily functions of respiration, digestion, and thus food intake, are closely related to changes in water temperature. During periods of extreme cold, for example, respiration slows down and feeding is greatly reduced. At the other extreme, when water temperature reaches about 75 degrees F, the pike suffers heat stress and again reduces food intake. However, between these two extremes there is a comfortable temperature range in which (all things being equal) the pike feeds at regular intervals. This ideal temperature range varies from one part of the country to another, but in my experience on the Yorkshire waters a range between about 55 and 65 degrees F seems best. These temperatures often coincide with early June and late September, both times at which the fish feed better – in my experience – than at any other time of year. In the following account I present a month by month record of the way in which angling results have been related to weather conditions. It is based on my angler's log and diaries going back over nineteen years.

Whenever I search through my old angler's log there is always one month which stands out from the rest. That month is June. June is not normally a month associated with pike fishing, yet on all the waters I have fished, and regardless of baits used, I have had more success with big and small pike at this time than at any other time. Of course June is a time of natural abundance: gone are the cold days of winter, the sun is out, water temperatures are fast rising, and the weed beds are alive with small prey fish. Temperatures are rising through the comfortable range and the pike are feeding hard to compensate for the energy lost during the spawning ritual. Scientists have also shown that growth increases in June, and this no doubt helps to account for the pikes' apparent hunger during this period. Following the early-season bonanza, late July and August can be less predictable months, characterised by high water temperatures which can stop feeding altogether, especially when temperatures rise above 75 degrees F. Under these conditions I have had disappointing results, regardless of baits or tactics. However, there are certain exceptions. For example, on the highland lochs of Scotland, where cooler conditions prevail, August heat waves can provide conditions which are ideal for loch fishing. These cold water lochs then enjoy conditions similar to those found in June back in England.

During the long hot days of August I suspect the pike become shade-loving creatures – in contrast with their sun-seeking habits of May/June. This may explain why they seem to shy off to the deeper pools. Bill McEwan has said that he prefers to pike fish on sultry days when there is a cloud ceiling – and, sure enough, such days do seem best in summer. However, of all the conditions which can prevail in August there is one particular set that can be relied on to bring good sport.

For many years now I have recognised the fantastic opportunities that accompany heavy rainfall or, better still, summer thunderstorms. Make no mistake, these conditions provide ideal circumstances for the river piker. Flood waters get those lazy summer pike fighting the current, forcing them up those easily identified feeder streams and areas of slack water where they can be caught in large numbers. Under these conditions the pike become unusually easy to catch. The floodwaters bring a useful combination of cooler temperatures, higher oxygen levels and cover which together make the pike feed hard, particularly in the rivers.

At the fall of the year our lakes and rivers gradually release their summer heat and provide conditions generally better suited to pike fishing. September brings the autumnal equinox (when day and night last about the same length of time) and this for many marks the start of the traditional pike season. During September water temperatures usually hover between 45 and 55 degrees F (the comfortable range) and conditions are generally ideal in both rivers and lakes. At this time of year I have found that conditions are compatible to those in June, in that sport is fairly consistent; mild settled weather improves prospects, whilst cold winds have an adverse effect.

Mild, settled weather is ideal in October too but sooner or later the first hard frosts appear and dramatically alter the situation. For many years I have noticed how the first cold frosts of winter cause a temperature shock which kills the pike fishing stone dead on the Yorkshire rivers. It seems to be a shock which ruins sport until February. Fortunately, though, this does not seem to happen on the deeper gravel pits and lakes where pike can still be caught when air temperatures are well below freezing point. In fact, sudden cold snaps drive these lake pike into the easily identified deeper water where they can acclimatise in the lower layers of warmer water. Such warm layers of water do not exist in the rivers and this may explain why sudden temperature changes affect the river fish so badly. They have nowhere to adjust gradually.

November and December often bring the first really cold air masses which quickly cool most waters down to their normal winter temperatures, which can vary from 32 degrees F to about 45 degrees F. Conditions are naturally bleak, yet unseasonally mild weather can dramatically improve prospects.

On 28 November 1979 a strong south-westerly wind (20 mph, 68 degrees F) caused the water temperature of my local lake to rise at a time when it would normally be falling. On that day I took several good pike up to 20 lb. The following day more doubles came to the net, including a very fat 23 lb fish, all taken on drifted sprat baits. The steadily rising thermometer had really got the pike feeding. However, soon afterwards the temperature dropped again. The following week brought two definite blanks and a lot of cold weather.

On 24 December 1968 Castle Howard Lake was ice bound except for a small hole next to the deepest part of the lake. By 3.45 pm even this ice hole was beginning to freeze over, but not before a lively 5-inch roach livebait was set beneath a 2-foot orange float. With air temperatures of 23 degrees F and a wind chill factor of about 14 degrees F the orange float disappeared and soon afterwards a beautifully conditioned pike of 19 lb 12 oz was lifted clear of the ice. Since that magical day I have returned to Castle Howard every single year in late December under similar cold conditions but have yet to match that December fish. Not surprisingly such consistently poor results cause me to rate December as one of the slowest months of all for sport, especially in very cold weather.

January water temperatues normally hover around 35 degrees F in Yorkshire yet despite such cold temperatures the pike continue to feed around midday. However, these midday feeding spells are feeble in comparison with the savage marauding of summer. In these semi-arctic conditions the pike seem to become comatose in the numbing temperatures. For this reason it is wise to fish sub-zero temperatures with low expectations. One or two fickle runs is all one can expect on the cold Yorkshire waters and once hooked, these super-cooled pike come in with scarcely a flutter of the tail – different indeed to their summer state. The truth is that in winter pike undergo certain metabolic changes which are induced by low temperatures. Generally speaking, the colder the temperature the slower and less active the pike become. Scientists have shown that food intake almost stops altogether in January, sometimes resulting in weight loss.

However, in late February and March the fish begin to feed again, despite cold temperatures. This is probably caused by some kind of hormone activity linked to spawning. Whatever causes it, there is no doubt at all that February and March can be extremely productive months.

Good fishing can be had in February and March after a sharp temperature increase. In March 1984 I visited Lindholm Lake and blanked with water temperatures just a little above freezing. The following week brought mild weather and by 10 March the water temperature had increased to 42 degrees F. This sudden amelioration of conditions caused the predators to start moving about on a heavy feeding binge and two of them came unwillingly to the net; together these two pike weighed 52 lb. This catch included a personal-best fish of 32 lb. After catching that fish I stopped fishing for the day even though it was only 8.30 am; had I stayed longer there would probably have been more, but it didn't seem important at the time. The following day found us fishing a small shallow, still water full of small pike. Seventeen pike came to the net. None of these fish weighed more than 2 lb 8 oz but it did show that the sudden temperature rise was affecting big and small pike alike.

Anglers who choose to fish during the English closed season often do so by travelling to Scotland or Ireland where coarse fishing is allowed all the year round. In these places some very big pike can be caught on the shallow margins as the fish prepare to spawn. Getting to the fish before they spawn is the difficult part; arrive too early and the fish may still be in the deep open water, arrive too late and spawning may have started already. Since pike spawn when the water temperature reaches 43 degrees F it is best to arrive sometime before this. In mild weather the fish spawn earlier than in cold weather so it is as well to leave the actual date of arrival to the latest time possible so as to avoid a wasted journey.

Numerous factors affect our sporting prospects. Air temperature is one of the most important of these as it has a direct bearing on water temperature which, in turn, fundamentally affects food consumption. Certainly if pike do not want to feed, for whatever reason, you cannot force them to. Obviously it is best to fish for pike when they are actually feeding, at which time there is a good chance of catching them.